AUTHENTIC

# Worship
### IN A
# Changing Culture

CRC Publications
Grand Rapids, Michigan

Printed in the United States of America on recycled paper ♻

1-800-333-8300

ISBN 1-56212-257-6

10 9 8 7 6 5 4 3 2 1

# CONTENTS

# ACKNOWLEDGMENTS

*Authentic Worship* is the work of many. It reflects the dedicated efforts of a seven-member Worship Study Committee that prepared a report for the 1997 Synod of the Christian Reformed Church. That report forms the core of this study edition.

**Duane Kelderman,** pastor of Neland Avenue Christian Reformed Church, Grand Rapids, Michigan, served as principal author. The council of Neland Avenue Church deserves thanks for granting Dr. Kelderman release time from his regular duties to devote to this task.

**Edith Bajema** is coordinator of worship at Oakdale Park Christian Reformed Church, Grand Rapids, Michigan.

**Wayne Brouwer,** pastor of Harderwyk Christian Reformed Church, Holland, Michigan, chaired the committee and ably guided its deliberations.

**David Diephouse,** academic dean at Calvin College, Grand Rapids, Michigan, served as secretary for the committee; he prepared the introduction and the discussion questions and commentary for this study edition.

**Lynn Likkel** is a church planter for Christian Reformed Home Missions in Seattle, Washington.

**Leonard Vander Zee** is pastor of South Bend Christian Reformed Church, South Bend, Indiana.

**John D. Witvliet** teaches worship, theology, and music at Calvin College and Calvin Theological Seminary, Grand Rapids, Michigan.

Numerous other individuals, both within and beyond the Christian Reformed Church, offered advice, critiqued elements of the report, or otherwise contributed materially to this project. To all these the church owes a hearty debt of gratitude.

# PREFACE

*Authentic Worship in a Changing Culture* began as a study report within one denomination, the Christian Reformed Church in North America. But the issues dealt with will sound familiar to many Christians in many different communions. Though the language is often "in house," we offer this study in hopes that other communions may also find some help in analyzing the theological and cultural landscape that is home to all North Americans.

When editing the report, one question kept surfacing: Just who is included in all the "we" language—the committee that generated the report? The Christian Reformed denomination? The broader Christian community? The entire North American cultural scene? To this multifaceted question, members of the committee usually had the same response: "Yes." In that same spirit, the committee did not speak of "Reformed worship," but rather of "Christian worship," acknowledging that "like every other worship tradition, the Reformed worship tradition has both received gifts from and given gifts to Christian worship; what it has given has arisen from what it first received" (p. 76).

It is our hope that many within the Christian Reformed Church as well as beyond will find this book helpful in understanding more of what it means to offer God our authentic worship in a changing culture.

Emily R. Brink
Music and Liturgy Editor
CRC Publications

# INTRODUCTION

```
BACKGROUND
```

Going to church is a way of life for most people in the Christian Reformed Church in North America (CRC). We take worship seriously and are worshiping in increasingly diverse ways. Gone are the days when a simple order of worship printed on the back of the Sunday bulletin sufficed to define the CRC at worship. Congregations are now experimenting with new forms of liturgy, different styles of music, and alternative ways of celebrating the sacraments. CRC worship, once resounding with a heavy Dutch accent, now has become an exuberant chorus of many "tribes and peoples." Leading worship, once a task reserved for pastors, is now likely to involve a broad cross section of church members as planners and/or participants.

This creative ferment has produced countless conferences and workshops, new denominational committees and publications, much study, and not a few arguments. What should happen in worship, and how? Are there right and wrong ways to worship? Exactly what is *Reformed* worship?

In 1968, synod adopted a landmark report on liturgy that sought to provide guidance on such questions. This report analyzed Christian worship through the centuries, outlined a biblical perspective on worship, and offered a number of models that many congregations today are still using with great blessing. Though not as widely utilized as it deserves to be, the 1968 report remains an indispensable starting point for reflecting on principles and practices of Reformed worship as we approach the twenty-first century.

Two contributions of this 1968 report are particularly noteworthy. First, the report proposes a helpful way of thinking about worship in general. The central thesis of the report states that Christian worship is a *dialogue* between God and the people of God. God moves toward us in revelation, and we move toward God in response. God comes to us in grace, and we respond in grateful obedience. The story is told, and God's people say thanks. While the concept of worship as dialogue may be open to refinement, the underlying principle remains a sound one. It provides a useful corrective to the conviction that worship is a purely human activity and that worshipers are merely passive spectators rather than vital participants in an active *engagement* with God.

Second, the 1968 report offers a helpful way of thinking about worship in particular. It identifies four core *motifs* (taken from the 1965 Synod of the *Gereformeerde Kerken* in the Netherlands) that provide basic criteria for evaluating and reforming contemporary worship. These four motifs are

- *the biblical motif (the Word of God)*. The Bible, although it does not prescribe an order of worship, is the church's basic orientation and authority for worship. The Bible reveals the God we worship and the kingdom established by the crucified and risen Christ. The Bible commands worship, shows us the Christian community at worship, and in its totality gives us the raw material for making certain theological claims regarding worship.

- *the catholic motif (the history of the church)*. The church at worship is organically connected with the body of Christ that has gone before and the universal body of Christ in the present. While tradition alone does not determine worship standards, this motif reminds us that the liturgy of the church is not ours first of all to do with as we please but belongs to the body of Christ. Respect for the enduring structure of Christian worship guards against individualism and gimmickry and helps us distinguish between the essential and the peripheral. History grants us an appreciation for what should be stable in worship *and* for what should be flexible and fluid.

- *the confessional motif (the faith of the church)*. Every church that gathers for worship holds certain beliefs, which it articulates in certain ways. Although formal creeds and doctrinal confessions may not be explicit in worship, what the church believes and how it worships should be integrated. The more self-conscious the church is about this connection, the stronger its worship and its beliefs will be.

- *the pastoral motif (the contemporary needs of the people of God).* A congregation always worships as specific people here and now. This motif calls worship leaders to ask, "Who are these people worshiping here today? What are their needs? What idols compete for their allegiance? How do they hear what is said?" While the other motifs are born of faith and memory and emphasize the need for stability, this one is born of love and expresses the need for flexibility.

Recently synod commissioned a new study to address the many dramatic changes in worship that have occurred since 1968 and that are reflected in the growing diversity of practices and attitudes found within the Christian Reformed Church today. The result is *Authentic Worship in a Changing Culture,* a report adopted by the Synod of 1997, presented here in an edition for study and discussion.

This report is not intended to be an exhaustive biblical/theological study of worship, nor is it a "how-to" manual for preparing worship services. At the heart of the report lies a theological reflection upon today's cultural situation in which we live and worship. It first identifies and explains some of the cultural forces at work in today's North American church and then reflects theologically upon these forces and the changes they initiate in worship. The goal is to equip church leaders with perspectives and insights that will help them make decisions regarding worship that are biblically and theologically informed as well as culturally discerning.

The central thrust of this report is a unifying one. "Worship wars" and labels such as *traditional* and *contemporary* unnecessarily polarize the church and unfairly caricature fellow believers' sincere attempts to worship God. This report strives to articulate a biblical/theological center for worship that resists simplistic either/or choices, one that embraces the strengths and critiques the weaknesses of worship at every point of the worship continuum.

---

### SUGGESTIONS FOR USING THIS STUDY EDITION

---

This study edition is intended for use by anyone with an interest in worship, especially for those who have direct responsibility for the worship ministry of the church (pastors, elders, worship committee members, worship planning teams, and musicians). Although the report occasionally uses technical language and style characteristic of synodical reports, it has intentionally been written to be thought-provoking and appealing to all church members.

The core of the report consists of two major sections:

- a concise summary of the contemporary cultural forces affecting worship,
- a more extended set of theological reflections on the enduring themes and contemporary dynamics of biblical worship.

Numerous questions, quotations, and suggestions for discussion are printed in the margins of these two sections. This material is intended both to stimulate personal reflection and to help prepare for leading and participating in group study. Some questions and quotations amplify specific points raised in the report; some are designed to connect theological principles and elements of cultural analysis; others are addressed primarily to those responsible for evaluating and renewing worship in a particular congregation.

The concluding section contains thirty questions and answers regarding typical issues individuals and congregations struggle with today. The purpose of this section is not to offer a definitive solution to every current problem or to anticipate every future controversy. Rather, the Q&A format is designed to model informed discussion of concrete issues. The goal of this section is twofold: first, to demonstrate how the cultural analysis and theological reflections presented in the body of the report can shape our approach to difficult issues; second, to emphasize that in controversial matters of worship, discernment and wisdom are as important as expertise in culture and worship.

This book can be used as a basis for individual study, for discussion in church councils and committee retreats, or as an adult education text. It is self-guided, and the material can be organized in a variety of ways to fit different needs and occasions. Two possible formats are suggested on pages 10-11. (Report sections and study edition pages are noted in parentheses.)

**Format One: A Two-Part Overview**

This format will provide a general overview of the report. The Q&A section (Section Three) of the report is not included here, although selected questions in the margins of the first two sections will refer you to this section of the report.

*Session 1: The Historical and Cultural Context of Worship*

• The 1968 Report (Introduction, pp. 6-8)

• Recent History of Protestant Worship in North America (section 1, pp. 14-19)

• Cultural Analysis (section 1, pp. 20-34)

*Session 2: The Dynamics of Biblical Worship*

• Enduring Themes (section 2, pp. 37-49)

• Contemporary Dynamics of Biblical Worship (section 2, pp. 50-75)

• Reformed Worship (section 2, pp. 75-78)

## Format Two: A Five-Part Study

This format will permit a more in-depth study of the report in a different order than presented in this study edition. It utilizes all three sections of the report and encourages discussion of local issues.

*Session 1: Looking Back: Historical Context*

- Reformed Worship (section 2, pp. 75-78)

- Recent History of Protestant Worship in North America (section 1, pp. 14-19)

*Session 2: Looking Around: Cultural Context*

- Cultural Analysis (section 1, pp. 20-34)

*Session 3: Looking Inward: Biblical Principles*

- The 1968 Report (Introduction, pp. 6-8)

- The Enduring Themes of Biblical Worship (section 2, pp. 37-49)

- Worship and the Heart (section 2, pp. 50-52)

*Session 4: Looking Outward: Community and Diversity*

- Worship and Community (section 2, pp. 52-58)

- Worship and Diversity (section 2, pp. 58-68)

- Worship and Evangelism (section 2, 69-75)

*Session 5: Looking Forward: Challenges and Opportunities*

- Selected Q&A (section 3)

- Local Issues

Obviously these formats can be adapted freely as circumstances dictate. Some proposed sessions and topics might easily be expanded, while others might be condensed or reordered. Parts of one format could be combined with the other—for example, a worship planning retreat might be organized on the basis of Format One but include a localized evaluation similar to the final session proposed in Format Two.

## Tips for Leading Group Study

When this book is used for group study, careful preparation by the leader is very important.

*Before the Session*

- Read the material carefully and consider how it relates to your particular situation. (While the general principles discussed in the report should apply everywhere, specific issues or examples may not apply to your church or group.)

- Review the discussion questions printed in the margins and select those most appropriate for your group. Jot down questions of your own; these are likely to be the most relevant of all.

- Arrange for someone to read Scripture and/or lead in prayer.

- Encourage group members to read and reflect on the material in advance.

*During the Session*

- Invite questions and comments from the group. You might want to set the context for a discussion by reviewing orally the relevant section of the text (or have participants do so, if they are willing).

- Pace the discussion so that time is allotted wisely.

- Respect everyone's views and give everyone an opportunity to speak. (Some may feel more comfortable expressing their ideas in smaller groups of two or three.)

- Assign people to follow up on questions your group could not answer or on ideas proposed. (At the end of this study edition is a list of resources for additional study and worship planning.)

We trust this report and study edition will be a source of insight and encouragement for all who read it. May the God from whom all blessings flow be truly glorified wherever God's people gather to worship.

# Contemporary Forces Affecting Worship

In the last thirty years the Christian Reformed Church has witnessed unprecedented changes in its public worship. Although the 1968 report of the Liturgical Committee was written to respond to increasing diversity in worship practices in the church at that time, that report could assume significant uniformity in CRC worship practices. Today that uniformity no longer exists.

The question in this section is: What happened? What are some of the historical, ecclesiastical, and cultural forces that have led to marked changes in worship in the last thirty years? We have chosen to answer this complex question at two levels:

- First, we offer a brief history of recent Protestant worship in North America.

- Second, we offer some analysis of our contemporary cultural situation.

---

**RECENT HISTORY OF PROTESTANT WORSHIP IN NORTH AMERICA**

---

Compare the four major forces outlined on pages 14-19 with the four motifs from the 1968 Liturgical Committee report (see pp. 7-8). How or to what extent do recent changes in worship reflect these motifs?

The 1968 report began with a brief history of Christian worship, a helpful outline of the major patterns of Christian worship with particular attention to worship in the Reformed tradition. Since 1968 four major forces have served as catalysts for change in Protestant worship generally and CRC worship in particular: the worldwide ecumenical liturgical movement, the charismatic movement, "front door evangelism," and cultural diversity.

### 1. Worldwide Ecumenical Liturgical Movement

The first catalyst for change has been the influence of the worldwide ecumenical liturgical movement of the last fifty years, which has involved scholars and church leaders across many denominations in an effort to promote worship renewal based on examples from the early church (second through fourth centuries). In fact, the 1968 report already reflects this influence with its call for congregational participation, the unity of Word and Table, and the recovery of the ancient pattern of thanksgiving at the Lord's Supper. This movement, which should not be confused with *high church* worship, upheld the following goals:

• to open up the riches of the gospel in worship, with particular attention to the death and resurrection of Christ;

• to encourage the "full, conscious, and active" participation of the congregation in worship (defined as follows by the *Constitution on the Sacred Liturgy* of the Roman Catholic Church and adopted by Vatican II in 1963):

"*Christ's faithful . . . should be instructed by God's word and be nourished at the table of the Lord's Body. They should give thanks to God. . . .Through Christ, the Mediator, they should be drawn day by day into ever more perfect union with God and each other, so that finally God may be all in all*" (Flannery, Vatican Council II: The Conciliar and Post Conciliar Documents, *pp. 16-17).*

The reforms of Vatican II have exerted enormous influence on worship renewal among Catholics and Protestants alike. Do you consider the Vatican's definition of "full, conscious participation" valid? Does it describe the worship in your church? Should it? Why or why not?

• to recover the ancient pattern of Word and Table as the normal pattern for Sunday worship.

Out of these goals have reemerged the following worship practices:

• the Christian year as an annual narrative recalling of events in salvation history;

See Q&A 25, pages 97-98.

- the *Revised Common Lectionary* as a way of promoting the reading of significant portions of Scripture in worship and in preaching the "whole counsel of God";

- an emphasis on expository sermons;

- the recovery of the ancient prayer of thanksgiving as part of the liturgy of the Lord's Supper.

Reflect on your personal experiences of worshiping in other churches and traditions. What, if any, evidence of the four major forces described on pages 14-19 did you note?

These liturgical reforms have been widely adopted, though in varying degrees, throughout Protestant and Roman Catholic churches. The official published worship resources of many Episcopal, Lutheran, Methodist, and Presbyterian denominations all have in varying degrees reflected these practices, often borrowing liturgical texts, hymns, and patterns from each other. For the Christian Reformed Church, some of these priorities, such as expository preaching, are not new. Others, like the use of the full prayer of thanksgiving at the Lord's Supper, are a recovery of practices of the early church but are essentially new to the experience of most Christian Reformed congregations.

## 2. Charismatic Movement

Second, worship in nearly every Christian tradition has been influenced by the charismatic movement. A series of revivals in the late 1960s, which resembled the earlier Pentecostal outpourings at the beginning of the twentieth century, soon led to important changes in weekly congregational worship. Like the liturgical movement, the charismatic movement has emphasized the active participation of all people in worship through active use of the body. Particularly characteristic of the charismatic movement has been the use of both contemplative and exuberant songs of praise and prayer, services of healing, times for ministry and prayer among small groups of worshipers, and (in some settings) speaking in tongues.

Closely related to (and perhaps a second generation of) the charismatic movement is the praise-and-worship movement, which emphasizes exuberant praise as one of the most important acts of worship. It is marked by the use of several simple scripture songs or praise choruses, a sequence of actions that leads the congregation from more exuberant praise to more contemplative worship, and the use of a team of lay worship leaders.

### 3. "Front Door Evangelism"

Third, there has been a growing movement to consider public worship to be a primary vehicle for evangelism, to promote what is called "front door evangelism." Only in the last fifteen years have many churches thought of worship as strategic in the evangelistic task. In the 1990s, however, the weekly public gathering of the church has been considered by more and more churches as one of the primary opportunities for evangelism (a new strategy for many congregations but not new for most evangelical congregations). Particularly influential in this movement have been church-growth experts Carl George and Donald McGavran, market analysts George Barna and Lyle Schaller, and pastors Bill Hybels and Robert Schuller. This broad movement has encouraged congregations both to make worship services more accessible to non-Christians and to plan events specifically to address the needs and concerns of non-Christians. This movement has used the resources of sociological analysis to identify the particular shape of North American culture. As a result, an entirely new terminology for worship has been developed: seeker-sensitive worship, seeker-driven worship, boomer worship, buster worship, and so on.

See Q&A 10-11, pages 88-89.

## 4. Cultural Diversity

Review the hymnal(s) your church uses for examples of texts and music from different traditions. How often do you make use of these multicultural resources in worship?

Fourth, cultural diversity has enriched worship for Christians of all backgrounds and traditions. Following the pattern of most denominations, the Christian Reformed Church has experienced growth in cultural diversity both in the denomination as a whole and within individual congregations. Worship in the Christian Reformed Church in North America is now offered in twelve languages each week. Diversity has led to the sharing of musical and textual resources among cultural traditions, exemplified by the fact that nearly every hymnal published in the past decade contains music from six continents and many North American cultures.

Today a congregation's worship style may have more in common with churches in a different tradition than it does with others in the same tradition. Is this a cause for concern or for celebration?

Importantly, all four of these movements have been reflected in and shaped by the market forces of the publishing industry. Through the first two-thirds of this century, many Christians relied almost solely on denominationally approved texts and materials provided by the denominational publishing ministries. Now congregations look for worship materials— including prayer texts, songs, hymns, and dramatic scripts—from large independent publishing companies as well as from denominational sources. At one level, this is an ecumenical movement of sorts. Christian Reformed congregations now learn from and are enriched by the contributions of a wide range of other Reformed, mainline, and evangelical churches and movements. On another level, this has meant that CRC congregations are subject to the influence of an aggressive, market-driven publishing industry.

"We marvel that the Lord gathers the broken pieces to do his work, and that he blesses us still with joy, new members, and surprising evidences of unity. We commit ourselves to seeking and expressing the oneness of all who follow Jesus" (*Our World Belongs to God*, 43; in *Psalter Hymnal*, p. 1032). How do these words apply to worship?

Certainly none of these developments is completely isolated from the others. Worship in a particular congregation may reflect the influence of several of them. The congregation may use praise choruses, celebrate the Christian year, and sing hymns from Africa and Asia. In fact, when historians look at most churches of our day, they may identify eclecticism, or what Robert Webber has called "convergence worship," as the central feature of much public worship at the end of the twentieth century among North American Protestants.

Worship in the Christian Reformed Church reflects the influence of all of these movements. Indeed, there has been greatly increased attention to public worship as a central activity of the denomination. The past thirty years have witnessed these activities:

- the publication of a new *Psalter Hymnal* and the launching of *Reformed Worship*—both of which are widely used and respected well beyond the CRC.

- a flurry of synodically approved liturgical forms. (New forms were approved by synods of 1971, 1976, 1978, 1981, 1982, 1986, 1991, 1994.)

- yearly conferences on worship-related issues sponsored by denominational agencies and educational institutions.

Particular changes in worship in the Christian Reformed Church include

- increased involvement of laity in planning and leading worship,

- growing adaptation or even abandonment of synodically approved liturgical forms,

- increasing diversity in musical styles.

"Each church has a prejudice—be it liturgical, traditional Protestant, creative, or praise tradition worship—that biases it against other worship traditions. But lately congregations are talking with one another. . . . At the same time, they are entering into dialogue with the historical tradition of the church as a whole. Resulting from this new relationship is a convergence of worship traditions. A spirit of oneness and openness is bringing the church together in a new experience of worship" (Webber, *Signs of Wonder*, p. 5). **What are your biases about worship? What evidence do you sense of oneness and openness in your church's worship experience?**

Identify the most important ways in which your church's worship has changed over the years. Have any of the four major forces mentioned in this section influenced your current practice? How? If you belong to a new or emerging congregation, what is your basic approach to worship? How was/is this determined?

As we reflected upon the Christian Reformed Church in the contemporary North American cultural situation, we noted six characteristics of that culture that are particularly significant in their impact on worship. As participants in North American culture, we fit, we buy, we change, we watch, we feel, we hurt. (Sometimes in what follows *we* refers to ourselves as members of the Christian Reformed Church; other times *we* refers to ourselves as members of the North American society as a whole.)

## 1. We fit.

**Does this description fit your church? If possible, compare the impressions of newcomers with lifelong members' recollections of the church a generation or two ago. How has the character of the church changed? Are any basic attitudes and values different? If so, why have they changed?**

In the past fifty years, a historically Dutch Christian Reformed Church has rapidly become culturally assimilated. Typical CRC members in the 1940s were very aware that they were Dutch, and they found their identity in a Dutch subculture that had considerable depth. Today that Dutch subculture is virtually gone in many places and is considerably less pronounced than before in other parts of the CRC. The wooden shoes were burned on the cover of *The Banner* in 1980. Some cheered. Some cried.

Many factors have contributed to the process of cultural assimilation:

• The barriers of language are gone.

• Many CRC members have participated in "the American dream" of material prosperity.

• Many CRC members have advanced to leadership positions in business, government, and community.

• Many CRC members have married persons from other denominations.

- Many CRC people have dispersed widely from insulated ethnic pockets out into the North American mainstream.

- CRC membership has become culturally and ethnically more diverse through evangelism and transfer from other denominations.

The result of these changes has been a much wider exposure to society as a whole and to other Christians and their worship. Though various ethnic groups within the Christian Reformed Church are at different stages of the process, this overall movement toward assimilation applies in varying degrees to most ethnic groups in the CRC.

Another reason why the CRC "fits" more comfortably in the North American church scene today than it did at an earlier time has to do with a broad shift in North American Christianity toward deemphasizing differences among churches. In the past, most members of a particular Protestant denomination in North America were capable of articulating what was theologically and/or historically distinctive about their denomination. No longer is that true. At its best, this shift is due to greater humility on the part of particular denominations and deeper recognition that the body of Christ is one (John 17). Energies are now spent on strengthening what unites us, not on accentuating what distinguishes us.

However, other forces are also at work. For reasons examined below, many North American church members (including members of the CRC) are less biblically and theologically literate today than thirty years ago. People today often are unclear about what they believe. Today's society values tolerance and open-mindedness more than it values discriminating thought. In this environment, most Christians are less

Suppose someone says, "People are less theologically literate today than they used to be because we no longer hear sound doctrinal preaching. We've become so preoccupied with making worship 'relevant' that we've lost sight of what's really important." How would you respond? What does Ephesians 4:11-16 suggest?

interested in and less capable of articulating what they believe and of identifying what distinguishes them from other traditions than Christians were before the 1960s.

Many congregations today prefer to call themselves "New Life Ministries" or "Grace Community Church" rather than "Main Street Christian Reformed Church." How likely is this to reflect or promote a loss of identification with the larger church? What are some ways a local church might work to strengthen its sense of identity with the church universal? Acts 13:1-3 and I Corinthians 16:1-4 will help you get started.

Curiously, at the same time that we observe this homogenizing tendency in North American culture and its effect on worship, we also observe a growing balkanizing or fragmenting tendency. At both the congregational and denominational levels, churches increasingly "do their own thing," with little sense of belonging to a broader, universal church. It used to be that churches were more like than unlike each other. That is less true today. At its best, this tendency is due to churches taking their mission seriously, identifying their "market niche" narrowly, and shaping everything in their ministry to reach a particular group of people. At its worst, this tendency illustrates the local church's loss of identification with the broader, catholic church. (Recall the *catholic motif* in the 1968 report that calls the church always to see its worship as connected to the broader, historic church—(see p. 7).

The important point to be made here is that, for better or for worse, the Christian Reformed Church now "fits" quite well into the North American church context. Fewer and fewer people take the *Yearbook* on vacation to find the Christian Reformed churches along the way. Even old theological enemies aren't quite the threat they used to be, and with that new open-minded attitude has come far greater exposure to other Christians and other ways of worshiping.

## 2. We buy.

We are part of a consumer culture. The shopping mall may be the most apt metaphor for North American society. Here is the grand meeting between consumers, who have a dizzying number of options, and sellers, who wield their sophisticated marketing research and advertising to influence consumer choices. Fully two-thirds of the American economy is driven by consumer purchases. At a profound level one can say the heartbeat of North American culture is buying and selling. As one person has observed, people in North America spend most of their lives making and spending money.

The consumer culture goes beyond just an exchange of goods. People buy and sell experiences, entertainment, dreams, and pleasures. Also, the marketing model permeates our society far beyond the shopping mall. Politicians determine their political convictions by listening to focus groups. Networks and radio stations determine programming by doing audience surveys. Even colleges and universities increasingly view their students as consumers.

**What is the difference between luxuries and necessities? How do the requirements of a modest lifestyle today compare with those of a generation ago? How many of the things we now regard as necessities are in fact luxuries?**

In this environment it should not be surprising that churches employ the marketing model. Churches are urged to think of themselves as shopping malls. Just as consumers prefer choices at the mall, so they prefer choices at church—in matters ranging from worship times to the variety of support groups available for various needs. Market sensitivity to what the consumer wants extends to public worship as well. Extensive research is conducted to find out what baby boomers or baby busters like or don't like. Beyond being merely descriptive, these market analyses often become prescriptive as well: if baby boomers don't like to dress up for church, then we must quit dressing up, the logic seems to suggest. A newsletter by Lyle Schaller that goes to all CRC leaders often subtly blurs the descriptive (70 percent of people don't like to hear the word *sin*) and the prescriptive (we shouldn't say *sin*).

At its best, of course, the marketing model applied to the church reminds us as congregations that we must know those we are seeking to reach and be intentional about reaching them. At its best, this is only a new wrinkle in the basic missiological principle that we must establish a "point of contact" with those we seek to reach.

At its worst, however, the church stands in danger of capitulating to a consumer culture by allowing consumer preferences to displace biblical or historical principles as the primary determinants of the shape of the church's ministry and worship. Moreover, an exaggerated consumer orientation to ministry and worship can be both the result and the cause of the church's losing confidence in its message and feeling inappropriately apologetic for being distinctive and different.

### 3. We change.

It is difficult to comprehend the rate and magnitude of change in North American culture. Technology has produced profound social change in the twentieth century. Our oldest living citizens can still remember a time when there were no automobiles or airplanes, not to mention telephones, televisions, or computers. That same technology, now driven by the computer, promises an even faster rate of change in the immediate future.

North American culture has a bias toward change. Deep in our psyche is the notion that change and progress go hand in hand. And reality hasn't tempered cultural optimism. We are always ready to try something new. Consequently, institutions rarely stand still and continually are defining and redefining themselves and their goals.

The North American penchant for change is accelerated by the mobility of our society. People move frequently, from neighborhood to neighborhood, from province to province. Traditions and rituals do not have time to take root and develop.

Moreover, North American suburbia does not foster a sense of place. Our place is every place. Put another way, we do not live locally. McDonald's, not the local butcher and baker, gives us our sense of place. Strip malls and subdivisions are more like than unlike each other in suburban Seattle and Sarasota.

Identify the major changes in your family, church, and/or community over the last generation. Have any older customs or traditions changed or disappeared? Have any newer customs taken hold?

In this environment of exponential change, combined with a loss of the traditional texture and depth of local communities, churches face profound questions about what it means to be a community of shared memory. How does the church build and nurture memory and continuity? In most churches, the pressure to change worship is at least as strong as the pressure to leave things the same. And the pressure to change what has been changed seems to increase with every change. C. S. Lewis in his *Letters to Malcom* (pp. 4-5) decribes this tension well:

> *A good shoe is a shoe you don't notice. ... The perfect church service would be one we were almost unaware of; our attention would have been on God. But every novelty prevents this. It fixes our attention on the service itself; and thinking about worship is a different thing from worshipping. ... I can make do with almost any kind of service whatever, if only it will stay put. But if each form is snatched away just when I am beginning to feel at home in it, then I can never make any progress in the art of worship."*

Is Lewis on to something, or is he just an old stick-in-the-mud?

Certainly there is nothing inherently wrong with change. In fact, we will see later that change is

According to some successful worship planners, one key to effective worship is to include plenty of unpredictability and keep people guessing; otherwise services tend to become stale, and people lose interest. What do you think C. S. Lewis would say to that? How *creative* can/should we be in our approach to worship? What do Psalm 96:1-9 and I Corinthians 14:26-32 suggest?

an essential characteristic of the church as a living organism. And no doubt CRC worship has often been unnecessarily rigid and inflexible. Yet healthy churches, like healthy individuals, also are able to take the long view of their lives and identify some level of narrative unity and coherence in their lives. If Jaroslav Pelikan's distinction between traditionalism and tradition is valid, namely, that "traditionalism is the dead faith of the living, but tradition is the living faith of the dead," the question becomes: How can we build positive, healthy traditions when we as churches seemingly never do the same thing twice with the same group of people? These are pressing questions in a culture that is ever changing.

### 4. We watch.

Here we have in mind the impact of television and the electronic media on society as a whole and on public worship in particular.

It is true that people have "watched" for centuries. Dramas and plays and games have long been with us. But the watching that takes place through electronic media, especially television, presents unique challenges and dangers. (We realize that there is a wide variety of television programming. When we speak of television and its profound impact on society and worship, we are thinking primarily of prime-time television programming and advertising.)

Obvious influences of television on Christian character include these three:

• The godless values of advertising and programming pollute values and distort beliefs.

• Advertisers understand that sex, money, and power are the three great gods of culture and spend millions to get television viewers to bend the knee.

- The overt and subtle messages of television pound away at the character of children of the kingdom of God.

Another way in which television affects Christians is that it subtly changes their way of perceiving and receiving stimuli and thereby changes their expectations about worship. Consider these effects:

- With its continually changing barrage of images, television shortens our attention span.

- Television raises our performance standards for worship. Before we heard Amy Grant, we thought Aunt Millie had a nice voice. Before we heard polished television preachers, we accepted the fact that preachers got a little lost in their thoughts from time to time.

- Television makes worshipers even more visually oriented than they are by nature. Consequently, propositions are out; dramatic sketches are in.

- Television conditions people to listen more intently when worship leaders touch upon a felt need in their lives and less intently when they don't.

- Television tends to make worshipers into watchers rather than participants.

In his book *Amusing Ourselves to Death,* Neil Postman takes this analysis a step further and argues persuasively that television and video media are part of a cultural revolution that is changing the very way people think and relate to one another. Postman argues that our culture is changing from a word-centered culture to an image-centered culture, from a reading culture to a watching culture. Reading involves analyz-

"If Christ were a musician instead of a carpenter, living in contemporary America, how would he make music? Would the industry allow him to show his meekness his way, or would a commercially palatable version of it be 'suggested' from which he would have to turn away? And in doing so, would he reject the bigger-louder-more-is-better artistry that seems to characterize so much of what we regularly take in? Then how would he hold his audience?" (Best, *Music Through the Eyes of Faith,* pp. 173-174). Is this a fair question?

ing, classifying, distinguishing, connecting. Reading is sequential, logical. Reading lends itself to discourse—the exchange of ideas. As Postman notes, it is very difficult to say nothing in a written sentence. Words carry meaning. The same cannot be said about watching, especially the watching that goes on with the electronic media. Pictures and images electronically manipulated "lack syntax." A picture offers no assertions to be refuted; it is not refutable. Images make an impression on the watcher. But an impression and persuasion are two very different things.

The shift from reading to watching, Postman asserts, has changed our way of communicating in modern culture from

- discourse to entertainment,

- substance to image,

- real relationships with real people to pseudo-relationships with television personages,

- ideas to information,

- wisdom to facts.

Postman adds this further dimension to his analysis of the impact of television on worship (pp. 122-23):

**Is Postman coming on too strong with his analysis of the influence of television? What do you think?**

*On television, God is a vague and subordinate character. Though His name is invoked repeatedly, the concreteness and persistence of the image of the preacher carries the clear message that it is he, not He, who must be worshipped. I do not mean to imply that the preacher wishes it to be so; only that the power of a close-up televised face, in color, makes idolatry a continual hazard. . . . For God exists only in our minds, whereas [the televangelist] is there, to be seen, admired, adored. Which*

*is why he is the star of the show. . . . If I
am not mistaken, the word for this is
blasphemy.*

This shift in ways of communicating—from discourse to entertainment—may help to explain a decline in biblical and theological literacy in our culture. This decline in literacy hasn't happened just because church members don't brush up on the catechism enough. It has happened because we think less analytically than we used to. In line with this change, analysts of public worship today note that people nowadays are less interested in ideas about God and more interested in experiencing God. The question for the worshiper in the nineties is not primarily: Was that true? but: Did I experience God?

It can be argued that the trends outlined above are in line with some much-needed correctives in the Christian church. After all, don't we need greater balance between a purely cognitive, analytical approach to truth and a more visual, narrative approach to truth? Between left brain and right brain? Don't we need a greater balance between head and heart, between Word and sacrament, between hearing and touching?

Indeed, those correctives are needed and, happily, are taking place in much of the Christian church, but the changes being wrought by the video revolution go beyond those correctives and challenge the very way we think about religion and reality. Ultimately Christians are people of the Book, people who believe in the power of words and ideas. Christians put their faith in one called the Word, and they believe that Christ transforms not only their hearts and wills but also their minds.

Peter Gillquist, once an evangelical pastor and now an Eastern Orthodox priest, writes: "Rather than set before her people a mere blank wall or wood panel or floral display, the Church . . . has historically displayed the icons of the Lord Jesus Christ and His heroic saints. These images, these windows to heaven, provide for those who worship Him the opportunity to see, with the eyes of faith, through the medium of paint and canvas to the Original. . . . It's time we capture our imaginations for Christ again . . . " (*Becoming Orthodox,* pp. 83-85). Are Gillquist's views in conflict with Heidelberg Catechism Q&A 97-98 (*Psalter Hymnal,* p. 906)? Does visual imagery have a proper role in worship? Explain.

What does it mean to be "people of the Book" where worship is concerned? How important is it for a Christian to be able to read? (Most, in previous generations, could not.) Do Protestants make a fetish of words? Do they misinterpret Paul's words in Romans 10:14-17; I Corinthians 1:20-25; and Colossians 3:16?

## 5. We feel.

It may seem odd to mention feeling as a significant cultural development. After all, people always have had feelings. Psychologically we know that feelings are an important part of a healthy and whole personality. In faith and worship, too, feelings are important and are minimized at our peril.

What we are referring to in this section is not feelings per se but our culture's absolutizing of self-fulfillment as the chief end of humanity. North American culture has evolved into what many have called a therapeutic culture: we are obsessed with feeling good about ourselves and about life. Increasingly we talk about issues in psychological terms. As evidence of this shift, witness the proliferation of books in what is usually called the "self-help" section of any general bookstore. Notice a parallel proliferation of books of this variety in Christian bookstores. The same shift can be noticed in what we call "news" today. The evening news used to report on things like a speech by the president or prime minister, actions by congress or parliament, and natural disasters. Now the evening news is much more oriented to the self-fulfillment concerns of its listeners. Regular segments such as "To Your Health," "Your Personal Finances," and "Retiring Happy" address the felt needs of the audience in compelling ways. While there is nothing wrong with these things in themselves, the cumulative impact of all these changes is to narrow the way people see life to psychological, therapeutic categories.

Does this description of television programming apply to the televangelism you are familiar with? To your favorite Christian TV program? Can broadcast media be used responsibly for purposes of worship? If so, how?

There is a powerful connection between our being a video culture (we watch) and our being a therapeutic culture (we feel): television programming is little more than the manipulation, captivation, and delivery of audiences to advertisers. Television networks exist to capture audiences. Their marketing experts spend millions of dollars to understand how audiences feel and what they respond to. Television producers know that North Americans are anxious, empty people. All programs, from the news to sitcoms to prime-time shows, engage people's feelings at levels far deeper than they realize.

The relationship of this therapeutic milieu to Christian worship is obvious. People who come to public worship on Sunday have had their felt needs addressed all week long by television, radio, and print media. These media have addressed these needs with breathtaking sophistication. Worship leaders can learn from these other media the importance of addressing people's felt needs. The danger is that Christian worship leaders will buy into our secular culture's preoccupation with feelings and self-fulfillment and will reduce the gospel to the self-fulfillment and therapeutic categories of that secular culture.

Of course, the gospel does promise self-fulfillment. But it is radically different from the self-fulfillment secular culture seeks. Jesus says we find our life when we lose it for him and his kingdom; we live when we die to self. This message has been "foolish" in every age. It is especially foolish in a therapeutic culture like the secular culture all around us.

**What should it mean when someone says, "I really got a lot out of that service"? Is this a legitimate response to worship?**

## 6. We hurt.

By global standards of wealth and health, it may seem odd, if not offensive, to characterize North America as a place where people hurt and suffer. Certainly people in every place and time have suffered. The issue here is not whether people in North America hurt more or less than people elsewhere; the issue here is the specific cultural character of suffering in North America in the nineties. The following five observations regarding suffering in North American culture are worth making:

**Compare notes on the local and national news of the past week. Do these observations about suffering ring true? What types of suffering are most common in your community and church?**

- **We're anxious.**

A prosperous society creates its own kind of anxiety, the anxiety of getting, of keeping, of spending. It has already been noted that North Americans use most of their time making and spending money. Activity so alien to how God made us leaves us empty and anxious. In terms of Abraham Maslow's hierarchy of needs, the primary locus of need in a prosperous society shifts from the need for basic security to the need for meaning, which, when not satisfied, creates psychic pain. Repeated studies of North American attitudes and lifestyles show that North Americans are not particularly happy or content.

- **We're broken.**

The breakdown of marriage and family has resulted in an increased number of people experiencing traumatic pain and brokenness within their own families. The broader erosion of community identity leaves individuals with fewer and fewer communal resources to deal with more and more personal and familial brokenness.

- **We are an addictive society.**

Substance abuse, eating disorders, gambling addiction, compulsive behaviors like workaholism—these are just some of the evidences of an addictive quality to much of life in North America. The craving to be "filled" with something, anything, testifies to an emptiness, a vacuum of meaning.

- **We are busy and tired.**

Often both parents in a family work outside the home. There aren't enough hours and taxicabs to go around. Our technology leaves us no downtime. We have cell phones, pagers, fax machines, answering machines, and e-mail. We are an instant culture. High levels of stress are accepted as the way of life in a technological society.

- **We are violent.**

An epidemic of street murders afflicts all of North America. More and more North Americans, particularly in large cities, grow ever more numb to the violence that besieges society. But there is also violence within homes and families. The violence of domestic abuse crosses not only national boundaries but also all boundaries of race, class, and religion.

What does all of this have to do with worship? When people come to worship, they bring with them all of these burdens. Our culture's permission and encouragement to feel our pain translates into people's wanting and needing to share their pain. In this environment churches rightly affirm the decision of many people to take their burdens to church. People come to church in search of healing and meaningful answers. They come to be lifted up and energized. Robert Schuller is helpful when he suggests that pastors and worship leaders should think of Sunday morning worship as more like an emergency room, where people come bleeding and injured, seeking healing, than like a lecture hall, where people come for cognitive adjustment.

Cultural analysis of the sort we have just engaged in tends to be overly one-sided—either too critical or too affirming of culture and its impact on the church. We realize that our cultural analysis above is primarily critical and cautionary and that it raises serious concerns about the effects of North American culture on Christian worship. At the same time, we have tried to avoid overgeneralization and to point out in each section ways in which these same cultural trends have not necessarily been negative. Our attempts to be balanced and fair are important not only for a constructive cultural analysis but also for the way we must talk about Christian worship.

"There has been a tendency recently to make worship an 'upbeat' experience. Lost sometimes in the happy atmosphere of services styled to make people 'feel good' about themselves and about God has been a sense of *contrition* or sorrow for personal and corporate culpabilities, and *lament* over the human situation" (Senn, *The Witness of the Worshiping Community,* p. 36). Is this criticism valid? Is true joy possible in the absence of lament? How can the two be balanced in worship? (See also Q&A 17-18, pp. 92-94.)

Do you consider the cultural analysis presented here to be balanced? What would you omit or add? What does it mean to be *in but not of the world* in the context of contemporary culture?

The preceding historical and cultural analysis is helpful but inadequate by itself. We now turn to biblical and theological reflection upon the preceding matters and upon Christian worship [Section Two].

# Theological Reflection

Compare this approach with the *regulative principle* observed by some Reformed churches, which holds that only those acts of worship explicitly commanded in Scripture are permissible. Does it make a difference whether one looks to the Bible for specific guidelines or for *enduring themes?* Should it? In this context, refer to Psalm 98:1. Why should we sing a new song according to the Psalmist? Is God still doing new things? Should that have an impact on worship?

In this section we will first set forth some of the *enduring themes of biblical worship.* Scripture is the foundation of all theological reflection upon worship. All conduct, including our communal acts of worship, is to be regulated by the principles of the Word of God. As the themes of biblical worship are developed, it will become apparent that our approach to Scripture does not focus only on those isolated passages of Scripture that speak explicitly of worship practices. Rather, our approach is a broad redemptive/ historical one which seeks to discern how the worship of the church is shaped and informed by the mighty acts of God as a whole, as those acts of God are revealed in Scripture.

After we have set forth eleven enduring themes of biblical worship, we will seek to address those themes to our contemporary cultural situation. Our discussion of the *contemporary dynamics of biblical worship* will be organized under the following four rubrics:

• worship and the heart,

• worship and community,

• worship and diversity,

• worship and evangelism.

We will suggest that the order of these four rubrics is important. Worship is first of all a matter of the heart. When God's people worship (first) with pure hearts and (second) in authentic community, and (third) when that community is ever renewing and being renewed in its worship, then (fourth) effective evangelism, i.e., the proclamation of the good news of Jesus Christ to those outside the community of faith, is the natural outgrowth.

Finally, we will address the question of *Reformed worship.* Synod specifically mandated this committee to identify the "nonnegotiables" of Reformed worship and to suggest ways the Christian Reformed Church can retain (or recover) the "Reformed character" of worship. The question of what Reformed worship is will be briefly explored.

---

**THE ENDURING THEMES
OF BIBLICAL WORSHIP**

---

### 1. We Were Made to Worship

All human beings are worshipers. Though it is true that not all people show up at church on Sunday morning, all people do have the capacity and the tendency to acknowledge that someone or something else is greater than they—worth more—and to praise and submit to it. When people worship in this most general sense, they not only express the worth of the other; they acknowledge their own dependency and need: I am unworthy; you are worthy. I am small; you are great. I am not complete in myself and desire you, the one I worship, to the point of giving myself to you. This is the dynamic, the rhythm, of worship in its most generic sense.

As Christians, we believe that the triune God, revealed in Scripture, is alone worthy of worship. Further, we believe that God has created us in his image, thereby making communication and relationship with this God possible and natural. We were made to worship.

### 2. Sin Misdirects Worship

Our fall into sin did not take away our urge to worship or destroy our sense of dependency. But it did misdirect our worship. We still bow down and surrender ourselves, but now we surrender ourselves to things and beings less than God. And whereas perfect surrender to the true God gives perfect freedom to the worshiper, surrender to anything less than God enslaves and

Eastern Orthodox theologian Alexander Schmemann describes secularism as "above all a *negation of worship* . . . not of God's existence [but of] man as a worshiping being, as *homo adorans*." Schmemann concludes from this that trying to make worship "relevant" to a secular society "is a hopeless dead end, if not outright nonsense" (*For the Life of the World*, pp. 118-119). Do you agree? What makes worship relevant?

What forms of misdirected worship are most widespread in today's world? In light of Exodus 20:4, is it possible that worship itself might reflect the creature instead of the Creator? Is this a serious problem for the contemporary church?

Some seeker-oriented churches intentionally design Sunday services for nonmembers and hold worship services for members on a weekday. Is this justifiable? Is it advisable? How important is it for corporate worship to be on Sunday?

diminishes the worshiper. As Harold Best puts it in *Music Through the Eyes of Faith,* when we worship the creature instead of the creator, slavery replaces adoration, addiction replaces hunger, blindness replaces sight, and works replace faith.

### 3. Life as Worship and Public Worship

The Bible often speaks of worship as the total life response of the Christian. Our whole life is a sacrifice of praise and worship to God for what he has done in Jesus Christ. As Reformed Christians who emphasize the lordship of Christ over all of life, we appreciate the sense in which worship is not limited to a couple of hours on Sunday. But the Bible also speaks more narrowly of what we might call the official, public worship of the gathered community, and it is in this latter sense that we discuss worship in this report. *Liturgy* is a term used to describe the more formal, corporate, public worship of the church.

### 4. Christian Worship and the Trinity

Christian worship is rooted in the triune God. The trinitarian character of worship has been understood in various ways:

- worship as offered to the Father through the Son and in the Spirit,

- or to the Father, to the Son, and to the Spirit,

In practice, most traditions are tempted to overemphasize a particular person of the Trinity. Is this a problem for Reformed churches? If so, where is imbalance most likely to arise? Why? What is required to maintain a proper trinitarian balance in worship?

- or to the one triune God.

Beyond these differences in formulation is the truth that God the Father, God the Son, and God the Holy Spirit are all vitally involved in Christian worship. It is through Christ that we have access to the Father by one Spirit (Eph. 2:18). In Romans 8 Paul speaks of Christ who prays for us at the right hand of the Father (v. 34), and the Spirit who intercedes for us when we don't know what to pray (vv. 26-27). Only the

Spirit enables us to know God as Father (Gal. 4:6) and to confess Jesus as Lord (1 Cor. 12:3). Christian worship engages us with the triune God—Father, Son, and Holy Spirit.

## 5. Worship as Dialogue

Along with the 1968 liturgical report, we as a committee affirm the dialogical character of Christian worship. Indeed, Christian worship takes place in the context of a dialogue between God and his people. However, we are aware of at least two ways in which the concept of worship as dialogue has been misunderstood. The first is to understand dialogue too literally. Saying that worship is dialogue doesn't mean that one can take each sentence uttered in a worship service and categorize it as either God speaking to his people or his people speaking to God. Such a schema becomes even more problematic when we try to assign roles to the minister and the people. The fact is that sometimes the minister speaks for God, other times for the people. Sometimes the people utter the Word of God; other times they are responding to that Word. Worship is not merely a script with only two parties speaking. To avoid this misunderstanding, we will in this report speak of worship as "engagement with God."

"Worship in God's covenant community is a meeting between a Person and persons, as it had been from the beginning. . . .The dialogue is the inherent structure of worship. The question of liturgy is the question of how the dialogue is appropriately and effectively articulated" (*Report of the Liturgical Committee,* 1968). Can you find a "dialogue" in Psalm 117?

A second way in which the concept of worship as dialogue has been misunderstood is in the underemphasis on the horizontal, communal dimension of Christian worship. In characterizing worship as dialogue between God and his people, it has become common to underemphasize the communal character of Christian worship. Worship is the activity of a gathered community organically united in Christ by the Spirit. The joy of Christian fellowship and the expression of Christian love within the body are not distractions from worship; they are integral to worship. Christian worship is rooted in

"Love that releases all of the heart's adoration, expresses all of the soul's attitudes, explains all of the mind's determination, and utilizes all of the strength of the worshipper's body is worship. . . . We must not be merely recipients of love; we must also be responders to love, for love must be communicated or it will die" (Cornwall, *Meeting God*, pp. 221-222). What evidence of this response to love do you see in your church? How can it include dialogue between the people of God?

covenant, a rich communion of relationships and commitments including

- the relationships within the Godhead,
- the relationships between God and his people,
- and the relationships among God's people.

## 6. The Larger Contexts of Worship

It's important to place worship in its larger contexts. Worship is an event that takes place at ten o'clock on Sunday morning on the corner of Main and Central. But it is also part of a larger mosaic of addresses and times. We demean worship, we damage, and impoverish it unless we see that

- worship on Main and Central is organically connected to worship in storefronts and cathedrals, straw huts and underground houses.

- the worship of all Christian worshipers is organically connected to God's dealings with Abraham and Sarah, Rahab and the spies, David and Jonathan, Jesus and the woman at the well, Philip and the Ethiopian eunuch.

- worship is organically connected with the worship of Augustine and Anselm and Aquinas and with angels and saints gathered around the throne of God, past, present, and future.

Many so called "liturgical" churches express the communion of the saints through the use of icons and/or special saint's day celebrations. What do you think of these practices? Does your church adequately embrace the "church of all times and in all places?" How can worship avoid becoming too limited to the here and now?

We worship as part of the holy catholic church. We believe in the communion of saints. Christian worship is not merely something Christians go to on Sunday; it is a much larger reality that is truly breathtaking in its scope.

## 7. The Narrative Quality of Worship

All of this is to say that Christian worship is highly narrative and dramatic. In Christian worship we participate in the broad redemptive story God is writing. The structure of the church year—Advent, Christmas, Epiphany, Lent, Eastertide, Pentecost—is narrative in orientation. It simply tells the story of the mighty acts of God in Jesus Christ. The sacraments also have a highly narrative quality to them. Baptism and holy communion dramatically present Christ to us, not so much by "pointing back to" but by effectively "making present" the saving acts of God (specifically, the dying and rising of Christ). In this way the sacraments re-present Christ to us. Finally, the broad story of which Christian worship is a part also has future dimensions. In our worship we practice for eternity, anticipating that great banquet and the worship of the triune God that will take place around the throne of God.

If worship itself is narrative, what story do you think it tells? How is this story told? (See also Q&A 26-27, pp. 98-100.)

## 8. Worship, Sacraments, and Sacramental Worship

The worship of the church is sacramental. That is, certain elements from the stuff of creation make God and his saving work present to us in worship in ways that go beyond the spoken or written word. Calvin emphasized that in sacramental worship God stoops to human weakness. When Christians eat and drink at the Lord's Table and when they pour the baptismal water, God bends to human senses in order to make his salvation present and real.

Our confessions (Heidelberg Catechism Lord's Days 25-30 and Belgic Confession Articles 33-35) clearly call us to an understanding of the sacraments as both sign and seal.

*For they are visible signs and seals of something internal and invisible, by means of which God works in us through the*

*power of the Holy Spirit. So they are not empty and hollow signs to fool and deceive us, for their truth is Jesus Christ, without whom they would be nothing.*
—Belgic Confession, Article 33

James F. White in his book *Sacraments as God's Self Giving* (pp. 25-26) makes this statement:

*Protestantism has tended to neglect humanity's need for the visible and tangible, despite Calvin's warning that our humanity depended on such means. We have, instead, settled for a lopsided anthropology, as if words were somehow more spirtual than actions. Who can say that Christ's self-giving through bread and wine is any less real than through the words of the sermon? It is the same Christ made known through different means. . . .When we underplay a sacrament, it is the same as mumbling a sermon. In either case, the people are not fed.*

**Does White go too far or does he align with the Heidelberg Catechism and the Belgic Confession? Why or why not?**

What is enacted and sealed in the sacraments is union with Christ in his dying and rising, and all the benefits of union with Christ. Christians receive these benefits by faith and through the Holy Spirit. In the Reformed tradition, sacraments are not mere ordinances, something Christ told his people to do, but the powerful means through which God works his grace in human hearts, through faith. In other words, worshipers do not bring meaning to the sacraments by their thoughtful faith; rather, God works directly through the sacraments, and faith receives what God has to give in them. Put another way, sacraments are not merely symbols or ways of remembering what Christ did. Although as Reformed Christians we do not believe that the signs are transformed into supernatural substances, we do certainly believe that they, by the Holy Spirit, convey to us the reality of Christ's body and blood so that we can say, for example, that we do eat and drink the body and blood of Christ.

> Sacraments are truly named the testimonies of God's grace and are like seals of the good will that he feels toward us, which by attesting that good will to us, sustain, nourish, confirm, and increase our faith. . . . First, the Lord teaches and instructs us by his Word. Secondly, he confirms it by the sacraments. Finally he illumines our minds by the light of his Holy Spirit and opens our hearts for the Word and sacraments to enter in, which would otherwise only strike our ears and appear before eyes, but not at all affect us within" (Calvin, Institutes of the Christian Religion, Book IV, XIV, 7, 8).

**Is this the way you understand the sacraments? What factors might prevent preaching and/or the sacraments from becoming true "means of grace"? How might such obstacles best be overcome?**

In the Reformed tradition preaching also has this sacramental character. Preaching as proclamation of the Word of God is a Spirit-charged encounter with God, not mere lecture or instruction. Just as bread and wine become identity-shaping vehicles of grace, so too do the human words of the sermon, so that in listening we expect to hear God speaking.

Walter Wangerin illustrates the sacramental character of preaching in a delightful story he tells about an elderly woman in the inner-city congregation he served. Each Sunday morning she greeted him at the door after the worship service. Sometimes she would say, "Pastor, thanks for your teachin' today." Other times she would say, "Pastor, thanks for your preachin' today." For years Wangerin wondered why this woman called some of his sermons "teaching" and others "preaching." When he finally asked her about it, she replied, "Pastor, when you teach, I learn something; when you preach, I meet God."

**Describe times when you have been particularly aware of God's presence in worship. Is it possible to meet God in ways other than through preaching and the sacraments? How? What implications does this have for how we should organize and conduct worship services?**

There is a need to reemphasize the sacramental nature of worship. Many Christian Reformed Church members are not aware of the sacramental riches of their heritage and as a result tend to see sacraments merely as fitting symbols for what is declared already in the Word, a helpful way of remembering what Christ did. With this limited understanding of the role of the sacraments in worship, it is no wonder that in many places, sacraments are more and more marginalized. Most CRC members probably would be surprised to know that John Calvin actually favored a weekly celebration of the Lord's Supper as noted by this admonition from Calvin's *Institutues of the Christian Religion*, Book IV, xvii, 46:

**Why do you think most Calvinists tend to pay so little attention to Calvin on the issue of weekly celebration of communion? (See also Q&A 28-29, pp. 100-101.)**

*Plainly this custom which enjoins us to take communion [infrequently] is a veritable invention of the devil. . . . It should have been done far differently: the Lord's Table should have been spread at least once a week for the assembly of Christians, and the promises declared in it should feed us spiritually. None is indeed to be forcibly compelled, but all are to be urged and aroused. . . . All, like hungry men, should flock to such a bounteous repast.*

We are convinced that, as we grow in our appreciation of the Reformed heritage of sacraments in worship and of sacramental worship, we will also grow in our desire to celebrate the sacraments more frequently and more joyously.

### 9. What (Who) Makes Worship Happen?

A number of questions run through the preceding discussion of worship:

- Who makes worship happen?

- Who is the primary actor or agent in worship—God or the worshiper?

- Is worship primarily an activity of God or an activity of the worshiper?

It is tempting to think of the people, the worshipers, as the ones who make worship happen. Certainly the people are active in worship. But biblical worship also gives due weight to God as the agent of worship. God is the one who always has initiated the relationship between God and his people. God's sovereign kingdom is the basis of our relationship with him. God has done everything necessary for salvation and shalom. Jesus says, "No one can come to me unless the Father who sent me draws him" (John 6:44). In the Word and sacraments, God is spiritually present in the worshiping community. In all of these senses God is the effective agent in worship. It is to this prior and primal activity of God that the people of God respond in thanksgiving and praise.

Put another way, worship is not just something people do on Sunday in the same way they work on Friday and play ball at the park on Saturday. The worship service is a divine engagement, a meeting in which God is doing *before* his people are doing and *as* they are doing. Acceptable worship is something made possible by God. As Reformed Christians, we see this dramatically in the proclamation of the Word and the celebration of the sacraments, where God is spiritually present and working. This emphasis upon God as an active agent in worship leads David Peterson to define worship this way: "Worship is an engagement with God on the terms that he proposes and in the way that he alone makes possible" (*Engaging with God*, p. 20).

Church members may well be aware of passages such as Psalm 50:1-6 and Matthew 18:19-20 that point to God's presence. Would unchurched visitors be aware of this "engagement with God" if they attended your services? How?

Understanding the transcendent and active role of God in worship clarifies the nature of Christian worship and corrects a tendency of Christians to reduce worship to a human performance to be evaluated. Worship is not first of

Does this mean that worship leaders should avoid making a habit of reviewing and critiquing services? Read Malachi 1:8-14. Does "doing it well" matter? To whom? How should this evaluation be done?

Compare impressions about the connotations of such terms as *liturgical, traditional, contemporary, low church, high church*. Is there general agreement as to what they mean? Which of these, if any, best describe your church? Do such terms have value, or is it better to avoid them?

all a matter of how good the sermon was or how moving the praise band or choir was. Worship is not a performance to be evaluated. Worship is a living drama in which Christians are active participants, a meeting of God and his people, of heaven and earth. A person is either "in" the drama or not. Hockey and football thrive on spectators. Not so with worship.

## 10. An Enduring Structure to Worship

These theological emphases are not mere abstractions; they exert very specific influence on the form and order of worship. As in any act of communication or work of art, the *content* of worship inevitably is reflected in and shaped by the *form* of worship. We are not talking here about specific texts, such as the forms for the Lord's Supper. Rather, we are talking about the overall pattern of worship. Importantly, every congregation has some structure or liturgy for worship, whether traditional or contemporary, high church or seeker driven, whether printed out or not. Particularly influential in North America among congregations that often think they do not have a liturgy for worship has been the pattern enacted first in evangelistic revivals: preliminaries such as music, drama, and testimonies; evangelistic sermon; harvest/altar call. Seeker-services in many ways follow this pattern, replacing the overt altar call with a low-pressure invitation to return for worship or to join a small group.

A study of Christian worship throughout the history of the church and in many cultures reveals a striking, recurring pattern in the structure of Christian worship. This pattern, which in recent years has been adopted by most major North American denominations, reflects the worship of the earliest Christians in North Africa, Asia Minor, and Palestine. It has been adopted and transformed by worshipers in Central American barrios, small African villages, and large European cathedrals. It is also reflected in the sample services that accompany the CRC liturgical report of 1968. More importantly, this pattern of worship flows directly out of the nature of the church as Christ's body, a living organism brought into being by Christ's death and resurrection and sustained by his Word and Spirit.

This historic pattern is simple: gathering as a covenant community, proclaiming the Word, celebrating the Lord's Supper, leaving for service in the world. Notice the essential activities in each section.

Note that this historic pattern described on pages 47-49 is already observed by the church following Pentecost (see Acts 2:42). Compare this pattern with the revival pattern referred to on page 46. How are they similar? Are there any important differences?

### Gathering for Worship

The purpose of the opening of worship is to establish the relationships that public worship enacts and portrays. The most important is the relationship between God and the worshiping community. This is established through a biblical call to worship, the opening greeting, hearty praise of God, the heartfelt confession of sins, and the subsequent announcement of God's grace in Christ. Second and also significant are relationships among those who make up the body of Christ. These relationships are established through the very act of gathering in Christ's name and also through liturgical gestures such as the passing of the peace and/or mutual greetings. Prayers for the congregation and the world are often included in this part of worship.

The period just before the service used to be a quiet time for personal prayer and preparation for worship. Today it's often a lively time of greeting friends and visitors. What does each of these ways of gathering say about relationships between God and the worshiping community? Which do you prefer? Why? Does it matter? (See also Q&A 21, page 95.)

### Proclaiming the Word

In this part of worship, reading and preaching the Word are central. A prayer for illumination— a Reformed contribution—often precedes the reading and preaching of the Word. The reading of Scripture is in itself a significant act of worship. The sermon amplifies, extends, and applies the message of the gospel to a particular time and place. Appropriate responses—the

Hughes Old writes, "Preaching is like tennis: it has to respond to those sitting in the pew. . . . An alive congregation makes for lively preaching" (*Themes and Variations for a Christian Doxology*, p. 134). How do you react to this cause-

and-effect idea? Is a sermon necessary for the Word to be proclaimed in worship? (See also Q&A 15, 22-24, pp. 91, 96-97.)

Some people speak of celebrating *communion,* others of celebrating the *Lord's Supper;* still others speak of the *Eucharist* (meaning "thanksgiving"). What does each word emphasize? Do Paul's words in I Corinthians 11:17-34 warrant use of any or all of these? Explain.

See Q&A 30, pp. 101-102.

Compare a typical service in your church with the pattern described on pages 47-49. Which of the four aspects does the service particularly emphasize? Are any missing? How important or necessary is it to adhere to this historic pattern? (See also Q&A 13-14, pp. 90-91.)

recitation of a creed, a prayer of confession and intercession, a song of commitment—follow the reading and preaching of the Word.

## Celebrating the Lord's Supper

The Lord's Supper is celebrated with joyful thanksgiving for God's saving work in Christ, with fervent prayers for the presence of the Holy Spirit, and with meditation on the work of God in Christ, past, present, and future. Often such meditation is focused on the biblical themes central to a particular sermon or season.

## Going Out to Serve

The final acts of worship focus on leaving the worship service for service in God's world. The service concludes with acts of dedication to the ministry of the church (including offerings of money and announcements regarding congregational ministries) and with the assurance of Christ's blessing for life in the world.

The Christian Reformed Church has never dictated a particular order or pattern for worship, nor are we doing so in this report. But this pattern historically and theologically recommends itself as a simple but powerful way to portray each week the fullness of the gospel of Christ and to elicit the full, conscious, and active participation of all worshipers. It is also a helpful standard for evaluating worship in local congregations. Comparing the worship of a local congregation to this broad pattern quickly identifies which aspects of worship are particularly weak or strong in the local church. As congregations continue to strive for spiritually vital public worship, we recommend this historic pattern for use. It embodies each of the emphases in the theology of worship presented in this report. It is biblically, historically, and confessionally sound, and it allows for pastoral sensitivity to the needs of local congregations. In short, it meets the four criteria for worship described in the 1968 CRC liturgical report and reiterated above. Finally, this pattern should not be seen as stifling creativity in worship. Quite the contrary. Just as in jazz, free expression depends upon structure before freedom can emerge, so it is with this fourfold pattern of worship. The fourfold pattern provides the structure within which freedom and creativity can emerge.

## 11. Worship Space

All the dimensions of worship that we have been discussing should be reflected in the worship space, the place where worship takes place. The physical setup in which we worship can be an enhancement to or a distraction from Christian worship. The central and elevated location of the pulpit in most Christian Reformed churches communicates the centrality of the Word and of preaching in worship. The communion table and baptismal font communicate the prominent role of sacraments in worship. Seasonal decorations and liturgical colors are important ingredients in shaping and defining worship. Open areas in the front of the church for lay participation in worship reflect an expansion of congregational space (not performance space) and corresponding expansion of the understanding of the role of the whole body of Christ in worship leadership and participation. Decisions regarding the acoustics of a sanctuary reflect various values and priorities. Flexible worship-space seating that lends itself to fellowship and interaction among believers reflects an increasing emphasis upon that covenantal dimension of worship. We are heartened by what we perceive to be heightened sensitivity in many Christian Reformed churches to the significance of worship space for defining and shaping Christian worship.

What elements of the worship setting particularly enhance your own participation in worship? Are there any major sources of distraction? If so, what, if anything, might be done about them?

"The whole history of church building is the history of compromises between arrangements best for speaking in God's name and those best for touching in God's name.... We need both a synagogue and an upper room for Christian worship. We need space in which we can both project our voice and reach out our hands. ... But our reach is limited by arms that, unlike our voice, no microphone can stretch" (White, *Introduction to Christian Worship*, pp. 91-92).

How does one go about evaluating Christian worship today? What is right worship? What kind of worship does God love? We will organize our discussion of the contemporary dynamics of biblical worship under four rubrics: worship and the heart, worship and community, worship and diversity, and worship and evangelism.

## 1. Worship and the Heart

Right worship is first of all a matter of the heart. In Christian worship God seeks people who love him with all their heart and love one another as they love themselves. Put negatively, God rejects worship of people who live divided lives. There must be integration between one's worship on Sunday and one's life on Monday through Saturday. Only then can worship have any integrity.

The prophet Amos ministered to people who had technically beautiful worship. They had been to all the latest conferences on public worship and could pull off breathtaking worship events every Sabbath. But after leaving services where they had sung of justice, they swindled poor people; after singing "not a mite would I withhold," they spent all their money on themselves to live in luxury; after saying they hated evil and loved the good, they actually sought evil and hated the good. God gives his evaluation of such people's worship in Amos 5:21-24:

> I hate, I despise your religious feasts;
> I cannot stand your assemblies.
> Even though you bring me burnt offerings
>      and grain offerings,
> I will not accept them.

*Though you bring choice fellowship
   offerings,
I will have no regard for them.
Away with the noise of your Songs!
I will not listen to the music of your harps.
But let justice roll on like a river,
righteousness like a never-failing stream!*

It is interesting that God goes into such detail in his description of Israel's worship. The rich and varied features of Israel's liturgy were not lost on God. But he rejected it all because there was no integrity, no consistency between what was expressed in worship and what happened outside of worship. In their worship they had the form of godliness but no power (2 Tim. 3:5).

When we as members of the CRC evaluate worship, we are tempted to focus first of all upon the quality of the sermon or the music. But God looks first of all for people who, having died and risen with Christ, are seeking to lay down their lives for the gospel, to serve God and not money, to love each other with deep kindness, people who come to worship expecting to meet God and leave worship determined anew to obey God. Nothing else matters if the worshiper does not approach worship with a heart truly seeking God.

Rev. Jan Overduin, a Dutch pastor, tells the story of his imprisonment in Dachau during the Second World War. In this concentration camp, inmates were not allowed to assemble in groups of more than three people. Public Christian worship was thereby forbidden. But the Christians there were not stopped. In groups of three, the Christians in Dachau would casually leave the barracks and trudge through the snow out into the woods. Standing in a small circle in the falling snow, they would first recite to one another as much Scripture as they knew, and then they would offer prayers to God. In later

Does this mean that worship is ultimately less important than service? Why or why not? Consider Nicholas Wolterstorff's claim: "If the works of mercy and justice are performed but the worship is missing, then a shadow is cast over those works, and *their* authenticity is brought into question. . . . God, whom we are to heed by doing the works of mercy and justice,. . . also requires of us that we celebrate in memorial for those deeds: work and worship are mutually authenticating" (*Until Justice and Peace Embrace*, pp. 156-157).

In what concrete ways can we express a "heart truly seeking God"? If worshipers can approach God in different ways, to what extent can a single worship service accommodate different ways of expressing this seeking heart?

"A pre-disposition toward the informal can unwittingly cultivate an insensitivity toward the One to whom worshipers come. . . . [but] pride is not superior to shallowness, and perceived superficiality cannot effectively be countered by labored efforts at being 'deep.'. . . However great my devotion to 'redignifying' worship, God will *never* be impressed by my 'worthy' efforts if they smack of a secret sense of superiority above the worship style of any other of his children" (Hayford, *Worship His Majesty*, p. 168). Which of these tendencies do you think presents the greater danger in worship today? Why?

Think of one or two worship practices that you particularly appreciate and one or two that you particularly dislike. Are there valid objections that might be raised to the things you like? Are there any valid defenses of the things you dislike? Are the differences involved a matter of taste or principle? (See also Q&A 1, 3, 9, 12, and 20, pp. 80-84, 87-88, 90, 94-95).

years Overduin called this "the church in its purest form." We could alter that slightly and say that this was the church at worship in its purest form. Christian worship will almost always be more detailed than what took place in Dachau in the snow. But it should never be less spiritually authentic.

This principle of worship and the heart applies not only to worship but also to discussions of worship. We deplore the fact that *worship wars* too often accurately describes how the church today talks about worship. We propose that no fruitful discussion of worship can take place if people's hearts are not right. When our hearts are right, we will refuse to be controlled by caricatures of the worship of those with whom we disagree. We will resist labels like *traditional* and *contemporary* when they are used to put down others. We will quit trashing denominational hymnals and traditions and quit using highly judgmental words like *ditties* and *schlock* to describe more contemporary music. We will not come to church looking for things with which we disagree in worship, but we will come to worship, regardless of what happens "up front" in a particular worship service.

This call to Christian love does not mean that there is no need to exercise discernment and judgment in matters of worship. Indeed, much of what follows in this report is intended to help the church become more discerning, more discriminating. But we are convinced from our own experience that when Christians' hearts are right, discernment and discussion among people of diverse worship orientations do not have to be destructive but can be enriching and can enhance the worship of the church.

## 2. Worship and Community

Public Christian worship is an act of the Christian community. The church as community is not an intellectual abstraction. It is real people in a specific time and place and with a unique history. Worship happens in the particulars of a gathered congregation with all its joys and sorrows. Biblical worship is always local.

By *community* we have in mind more than fellowship. Certainly fellowship—people knowing one another intimately and caring for one another deeply—is an important feature of the body of Christ and of Christian community. But by community we have in mind something deeper. Christian community is the shared identity we have with others in a particular time and place because of shared beliefs, shared meanings, shared values, and shared purposes.

Healthy worship and healthy community go together. Conversely, when the church as a community is weak, so is the church's worship. Put another way, strong worship both builds and reflects strong community. We will examine both the challenges to community and the formation of community.

*Five Challenges to Community*

Many things in our contemporary culture assault the church as a community. We have already examined some of them in our cultural analysis. Consider the following five cultural factors that weaken community in general and Christian community in particular.

- **We are a mobile society.**

Most adults do not live in the neighborhood and belong to the church in which they grew up. Church communities experience high rates of turnover in church membership. This contributes to a loss of shared memory, memory that gives depth and breadth to Christian worship. (It is also true that a congregation primarily comprised of people without deep roots and extended family connections in a local commu-

If biblical worship is always local, how can it also be an expression of the "communion of saints" in all times and places? In the Heidelberg Catechism Q&A 55 (*Psalter Hymnal*, p. 883), we confess, ". . . believers one and all, as members of this community, share in Christ. . . ." How might this confession help us answer this question?

Should it be possible for a person to "feel at home" worshiping with any Christian community, even one very different from one's own? Why? If so, to what extent?

Do the five cultural factors explained on pages 53-56 describe you and/or your fellow church members? What would you identify as the greatest challenges to community in your church?

nity often experiences richer and deeper community because its members have lost those other community connections.)

- **We live segmented lives.**

In a technological society, it is possible to live separate lives in several different worlds. For example, we have our world of church, our world of work, and our world of neighborhood, and there is virtually no overlap between them. People at work may not even know where their fellow workers live or where they go to church, much less be a part of those other worlds. Consequently, no one knows anyone else fully. We tend to know and be known in fragments. In community, in its fullest sense, we know and are known by each other as whole persons.

- **We experience brokenness.**

The breakdown of marriage and family is itself a profound breakdown of community and almost always leads to further isolation and alienation from communities that humanize and nurture us.

- **We are cut off from our past.**

The rapid rate of change in North American culture has a tendency to cut people off from meaningful traditions that give identity and fiber to community in general and to the worshiping community in particular. In decades past, churches occasionally changed the call to worship or the offertory prayer. Today churches tend to change many things and to change them frequently. In the past the pressure to remain the same was greater than the pressure to change. Today it is often the other way around.

Since the church is supposed to be constantly reforming, shouldn't we expect it to be always changing? What types of change do you think pose the greatest threat to healthy community? What changes could help strengthen community?

- **We focus on felt needs.**

Worship in a pervasively therapeutic culture puts tremendous pressure on the church to focus upon the felt needs of the worshiper (see

Section One—We feel, pp. 30-31). At its best, this is good inductive communication—begin where the worshiper is. The problem of the inductive model, when coupled with a highly therapeutic and narcissistic culture, is that worship often ends where it begins—with individuals and their needs as they define them. Worship comes out to the individual, but the individual is not drawn into the community.

Can worship address individual needs without becoming defined by them? If so, what might be some practical ways to do this?

To be sure, some congregations are not sensitive enough to the felt needs of worshipers. In these congregations, worshipers have to travel the full distance between their world and the world of the church. Congregations that don't help worshipers in this journey simply lose them. Worshipers don't come back because they see the church as boring and irrelevant.

An equal and peculiarly modern danger is that the church seeks to travel the full distance between the worshiper's world and the world of the church, and as a consequence the worshiper never moves, is never transformed by the gospel. As William Willimon has said so eloquently, the gospel doesn't just come to my world and meet my needs as I understand them. The gospel creates its own new world, and it radically redefines my needs. For example, I think my need is for more money, but the gospel exposes my real need: to be set free from the bondage of consumerism. The danger in a therapeutic culture is that we make people's perceived needs sovereign. A church that does so soon loses its faith in the power of the gospel to draw people out of their world into the new world of faith and the church.

In today's therapeutic milieu, people have little interest in and regard for the traditions of a worshiping community that have developed over time, traditions that give depth and fiber to community. The reasoning goes something like this:

"Provision of hospitality to the stranger is full of dynamic conflict. It requires a decentering of our self-centered lives that is most disturbing. . . . It means that we must be prepared to have the tables turned, to discover that we are the guests in need of hospitality" (Keifert, *Welcoming the Stranger*, p. 59).

How is new life brought into the worshiping community? Reflect on this answer in relation to your own church: "Not by throwing tradition out the window. . . . A green spring shoot . . . never looks fresher than when it grows out of an old tree that has been tended and loved for generations. . . . The church has been pruning our liturgical tree for a long time, and though there are wild branches, it is not really difficult to see the general shape of the main trunk. That is where we must look for the life of the tree" (MacGregor, *The Rhythm of God,* p. 10).

Take a second look at I Corinthians 14. What is the biblical meaning of *edification* as Paul sees it?

if I can't see how a particular liturgical act meets my needs today, then the liturgical act is worthless and should be discarded. But such a view of what makes a liturgical act valuable and important is narrow and superficial. Worship is bigger than my felt needs, and the impact of worship is more subtle than can be measured by my reaction to a given service. It's also worth noting here that we rarely get rid of liturgy. We usually merely replace one liturgy with another.

*The Formation of Community*

One of the formidable challenges facing the church of Jesus Christ in our day is the challenge of building genuine Christian community—the fellowship of shared meanings, shared joys and sufferings, and shared purposes that has its unity in baptism into Christ's death and resurrection, made possible by God the Father through the Spirit.

In his book *Engaging with God* (pp. 211-212), David Peterson observes that in 1 Corinthians 14 the Apostle Paul

*challenges the common assumption that church services should simply be designed to facilitate a private communion with God, either by spiritual exercises or ritual. [Paul] envisages that believers will come together for the benefit of one another, drawing on the resources of Christ for spiritual growth by the giving and receiving of Spirit-inspired ministries. . . . As the church is edified intensively—being strengthened, consolidated, and preserved as the community of God's people—it may also be edified extensively—being enlarged by the conversion of those who may be visiting or invited by Christian friends.*

Beyond techniques and programs the church must live fully out of the biblical vision of the body of Christ, where the church is not merely a human organization but is a divine organism, a living reality with Jesus Christ as its living head. The church must identify the ways in which consumerism and hedonism have so infected the church's life that the power of the church as a countercultural community, a community that stands over against these godless idolatries, has been dissipated. The church must hear anew the call of the gospel to leave all and follow Christ. The church must continually recommit itself to its mission, in which losing its life for Christ is the way it finds its life. The community that is forged in the suffering that comes from self-giving will produce a worship with strength and depth.

Think of contemporary examples of discipleship (Mother Teresa? a local volunteer program?) that have impressed you. How can worship celebrate or encourage such discipleship?

The church also must understand anew the strategic role of worship in forming community. The church is a community of shared memory and shared meanings, shared stories, shared beliefs, shared ways of praying and worshiping. As congregations contemplate changes in worship, they must do so within their broad historical picture. Churches that do so will also keep before them the community-forming and community-sustaining power of the sacraments of baptism and the Lord's Supper. Even when a church radically changes its worship, it must still seek a unity with its past and with the essential activities that constitute biblical worship.

Eugene Peterson talks about the crucial role of memory in a church's life. Unlike nostalgia, merely living in the past, memory is the capacity of the human spirit to connect the experience of last year with the one of yesterday and at the same time to anticipate next week and next year. The healthy church, just like a healthy person, has a rich memory and maintains some level of narrative unity and coherence in its own tradition even as it makes meaningful and some-

"Neither persons nor nations can exist in a healthy state absorbed in novelty and defined by advertising. We require a history of salvation and a hope of a kingdom. We need a past and a future that impinge on the present and give it dimensions. . . . Prayer develops these dimensions. Without prayer the past becomes nostalgia and the future fantasy" (Peterson, *Earth and Altar*, p. 86). How can prayer be used to provide memory for new members in a church community?

How can authentic worship help cultivate memory? How might this "memory" be different for African, Asian, or Native-American Christians and for Anglos? How should it be the same? (See also Q&A 6, p. 86.)

times radical changes in worship. Walter Brueggemann has said that the church in our culture is the antidote to amnesia. In an age when memory is not highly valued and in which the Christian church is increasingly losing its memory, the cultivation of memory is a formidable challenge but one worth heroic effort.

## 3. Worship and Diversity

The order in which we are discussing worship in this section of our report is significant, for only when our hearts are right and only when we are worshiping in genuine Christian community can we talk meaningfully about diversity, growth, and change in worship. "Growth and change" in worship becomes a code phrase for conflict if this order is violated. But when growth and change take place among people whose hearts are right and who are in Christian community, God is praised in ever-expanding and ever-deeper ways. We will discuss our appreciation of God's diverse creation, the importance of rootedness, the relationship of church and culture, the need for balance between old and new musical expressions, and the lessons we can learn from children's worship.

### Creation and Diversity

The starting point for this discussion is an appreciation of just how much God loves variety and diversity. The world God created is marvelously varied, with thousands of different flowers and leaves, stars and planets, mountains and meadows, fish and fowl. Variety and differences are not bad; they enrich the world as God created it. Variety is not to be feared but to be appreciated as a gift from a rich and generous God.

In his insightful book *Music Through the Eyes of Faith*, Harold Best reflects upon the diversity of God's creation and wonders how the same God could think up things as varied as a hippopotamus and an orchid, call both of them beautiful, and still maintain some internal integrity and unity. It's obvious, Best concludes, that God's sense of rightness and beauty is so large and all-encompassing that it can embrace objects and creatures of his handiwork that seem too varied and different to be classified together as beautiful.

In the same way, all Christians must begin any discussion of diversity and change in worship by acknowledging the staggering variety of ways in which God is worshiped. God's people gather in cathedrals and in straw huts, in storefronts and in underground houses. Musical instruments and the sounds and songs they produce vary greatly around the world and through the ages. The fact is that God is honored and worshiped in a multitude of different ways. The worldwide church itself is the strongest argument against and antidote for provincialism in worship.

**Read Psalm 148, and note how the psalmist calls all of God's creation to praise God. How important is it for individual congregations to reflect the diversity of God's people? Some church growth experts argue that churches are more likely to thrive if they are relatively homogeneous. Does diversity hinder or enhance church growth in your community? Revelation 7 gives us the biblical vision of what worship will ultimately be. How can we begin to move in that direction?**

At Pentecost God showed the breadth of his vision for the church as he gathered people from different nations into one body, crossing lines of ethnicity and race that had previously been thought uncrossable. In so doing, he made clear his plan for the ages: "to bring all things in heaven and on earth together under one head, even Christ" (Eph. 1:12). In God's plan the church is the showcase of unity and diversity. The church is as culturally and ethnically and aesthetically varied as the human family itself, but it is nevertheless one, organically united in Christ. All things hold together in Christ (Col. 1:17).

Christians do not need to fear diversity in worship. Living in the Spirit of Pentecost, they will seek out and welcome variety in the way they worship God. We can be enriched by and can grow through our exposure to the richness and variety of the church's worship.

## Rootedness

The call to seek diversity and growth in the worship life of the church is not a call to erase a particular worship identity or, worse, to apologize for having a strong worship identity. Best suggests that "centeredness—our sense of home and place—is the only legitimate context for pluralism." That is, churches must know who they are, and even love who they are, if they are to have the perspective and freedom they need to look lovingly into the worship ways of others and be nurtured by them. If they don't know and love themselves before they begin to reach out, they will tend to be either too uncritical or too judgmental of other ways of worshiping.

In this regard it is worth noting a discovery of many churches in urban areas. Churches in urban areas of America tend to be older churches with a strong worship tradition. They also tend to be churches that now seek to minister to people of various racial and ethnic backgrounds. At first glance one might think that churches in this situation would do best to deemphasize their own worship tradition and find the common denominators between their own worship tradition and the traditions of the people to whom they are ministering. But in fact there is growing evidence that this is the wrong approach. There is growing evidence that the churches that minister most effectively in urban environments are churches that know and appreciate their own history, have a strong "center" of worship identity, and expand that worship identity carefully and integratively.

There is a vast difference between embracing diversity and trying everything that comes along. Churches must understand why they do what they do and then carefully decide whether, when, and how they will alter what they do. Churches must see themselves as ships, not motorboats. The direction of a motorboat can easily be changed, but the danger is that a motorboat will quickly get off course. The direction of a ship can be changed only gradually, but when it is changed, its new direction is clear and stable. Exercising caution and care in worship change is not evidence of a lack of faith or a lack of vision or a fear of change. It is simply wise, because it takes the long view of how a church's worship identity evolves.

### Worship in the World But Not of the World

A difficult issue that arises in any discussion of change and diversity in worship is the relationship of the church to the surrounding culture. The church's worship is inevitably affected by the broader culture in which it worships. Should this be? Shouldn't the church transform culture and not the other way around? Why should church people bring guitars and drums into the church? Why don't they instead bring Bach into the shopping mall? These are good questions in any age, but especially in our age, when the secularizing forces of culture are very pervasive and powerful.

The simple answer to all these questions is that the church should not and need not be apologetic for ways in which Christian worship is different from the broader culture and must not accommodate to cultural pressures to change worship simply because accommodation is easier than resistance to those pressures. Indeed, the church is a radically countercultural and culture-transforming community. The church calls people into a new world when it calls people to new life in Christ. That new world includes new ways of worshiping, singing, and seeing all of life.

**Suppose someone said to you, "I went to a different church last Sunday, and it was great! In fact, it hardly felt like church at all. You've just got to come and check this out!" How would you respond?**

Having said that, we must also make some other observations about the relationship of the church and the world. These three observations are not meant to undercut the unequivocal call of the gospel to transform the world; they are meant to deepen understanding of the relationship between the church and the world.

- **The church is in the world.**

First, as Reformed Christians we should be sensitive to ways in which the dichotomy between the church and the world can be overstated. Indeed, the questions posed above assume a clear demarcation, but the line between the church and the world is not neat and clean. As Reformed Christians we take creation seriously. All the world is God's. God himself took on human form in the incarnation. Not only moral laws but also musical laws, artistic laws, and aesthetic laws have been created by God for all people to obey and benefit from. We use the term *common grace* to explain how the unregenerate as well as the regenerate can tap into truth and beauty in endeavors ranging from art to music to science.

The fact is that when Christians seek these laws referred to in the previous paragraph to exercise creativity in worship (for example, in art and music), they are doing so *in the world,* which is exactly what they are supposed to do. Since Christians work in the world, it is only natural that our ways of creating music in the church, for example, will be influenced by broader forces in the world in which we find ourselves. We do not create music in a vacuum. All music, including the music whose primary context is the church at worship, is created in multiple contexts, because composers live in multiple communities: ecclesiastic, economic, sociological, political, cultural, familial, geographic, and technological. Again, music is not created in a vacuum.

In summary, the point here is that there are ways in which music which does not have explicitly Christian contexts nevertheless influ-

*Does it matter whether the materials used in worship are produced by Christians? If you had to choose between trite materials produced by a Christian or something first-rate by a non-Christian, which would you choose? Why?*

*Suppose someone says, "Reformed people may talk a lot about transforming culture, but more often than not the culture ends up transforming them." In light of Matthew 5:13-16 and John 17:13-19, how would you respond? What implications does your response have for the way we ought to worship?*

ences Christians' taste in music—what they like or dislike, what does and doesn't move them—because the church exists in the world.

- **Musical contexts are always changing.**

Second, the questions on page 61 assume that history is static and that musical contexts are set in stone. But history is not a painting on a wall, where everything has stopped. It is a drama where things continue to move and develop.

Consider the contrast between the use of guitars and the use of the organ in worship services. Today, as opposed to thirty years ago, the musical associations for most worshipers are not as neat as "Bach equals church" and "guitars and drums equals sixties counterculture." Several generations of people have grown up in mainline churches where the gospel has been muted by liberalism and cultural accommodation and where the music of Bach says more about the socioeconomic and cultural strata of the worshipers than it does about their hearts. For those generations, "Bach equals the symphony and upper-middle-class culture," not "Bach equals church." Those generations have come to associate Bach with cultural Christianity, not genuine Christianity.

In the same way, guitars and drums do not so clearly equal the sixties counterculture. The sixties generation has grown up in an electronic age in which they have been exposed to a multitude of musical forms and contexts of meanings. There are nuances and differences within the musical forms. The simple equation "band equals sixties counterculture" has long broken down. Following a long tradition, Christian artists have attached Christian lyrics to musical forms also derived from rock bands of the sixties so that for many people today, especially those who are younger, a band with guitars and

A few churches still solve the problem of music styles by banning all musical instruments and singing only songs found in the Bible itself (for example, the psalms). What do you think of this approach? Is anything wrong with it?

"If our music . . . must all be 'religious,' every selection used in morning worship needing to contain references to God or Jesus or the Holy Spirit, or to sin or salvation, we are going to reduce our effectiveness as a mission. Will we not dare to sing 'The Impossible Dream' on a Sunday morning? Might it not be more suitable at a special moment than anything in the hymnbook?" (Schuller, *Your Church Has a Fantastic Future!* p. 94). What do you think?

drums may have stronger associations with Christian worship than the organ does.

In summary, musical contexts, and therefore the meanings people attach to particular kinds of music, are always changing.

- **The church's evangelistic calling raises questions about worship and musical forms.**

Third, the questions on page 61 do not adequately grapple with the evangelistic calling of the church. We will deal with the question of worship and evangelism more in depth in the next part of this report. It is sufficient to point out here that while the task of bridge building between the Christian and non-Christian world is a very difficult one and is fraught with peril for the Christian church, especially in a radically secularized culture, nevertheless, churches that take their evangelistic task seriously must struggle with the issues of worship and musical forms in an attempt to reach nonbelievers for Christ. Later in the report we will discuss more thoroughly what this does and does not mean.

*Old and New Musical Expressions*

What does all of this mean, concretely, for change in worship? It calls for balance. We must sing both the old and the new, love the tradition, and heartily embrace meaningful change. Let's examine both of these aspects.

- First, the church must continue to sing its own songs and sing them with power and passion.

In music, the church must sing its old songs without apology. Even though the surrounding non-Christian culture may not appreciate the musical forms of the church's songs, the church must sing those older songs with fervor, for they help define the church. Not to sing them is to deny who the church is.

On this subject, it's important to remind ourselves that the church's most powerful songs have always been the songs rising from its own experience (not those produced by religious publishers) and born out of the church's tears. *Soul* is a term some use to describe the quality of songs that were born in the midst of the church's suffering. The African-American church tradition is not the only tradition to have such songs. Every tradition has songs and sounds that are distinctively its own and that took on unique power in suffering. This brings us back once again to the importance of community if the church is to have a vital and vibrant song. As Paul Westermeyer has said, "The song of our worship grows out of a vision of community that transcends our brokenness and in a remarkable way takes sounding from among us as healing balm" (*The Hymn*, January 1995).

- Second, the church must not fear changes in musical expression and in fact must embrace changes—carefully, integratively, and pastorally.

As we have seen, we live in the world. Musical sounds of the culture in which we live are part of the air we breathe, especially in an electronic age when music can be transported everywhere we go. Christians who live in the world cannot help singing and creating music that reflects the musical sounds and forms around them.

But Christians must create their new songs carefully and integratively. Associations are born and die hard. We must be vigilant that we are indeed recontextualizing musical forms and not merely pasting Christian words on musical forms that are still so contextualized in anti-Christian settings that the music and the message are dissonant, if not contradictory. We must create our new song gradually. Too many

Suppose someone says, "Decisions about church music are far too important to be left to church musicians." Would you agree or disagree? Why? Who decides what music will be used in your church? What criteria apply? (See also Q&A 5, 7, and 8, pp. 85-87.)

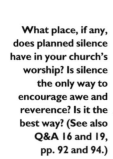

churches have introduced music changes violently instead of gradually. There is no excuse for inflicting musical violence on a congregation with a rich musical identity. Such musical violence is musically foolish because it does not help build the kind of narrative unity in the church's worship that is our ideal. It is also pastorally foolish. Worship leaders must remind themselves that people come before musical agendas. Worship leaders can be sensitive to the congregation they serve and still introduce meaningful, even if gradual, musical change. Large doses of wisdom, patience, and love go a long way to change worship wars into worship adventures.

*Worship and Children*

As we seek meaningful growth and change in worship, we will do well to look at our own children in worship. Many churches across the United States and Canada have developed strong children's worship programs in recent years. The genius of these programs has been the way they have tapped into the natural rhythms of worship that children so beautifully express. Tapping into the rhythms of children has, in turn, awakened many of those same rhythms in adults. Children's worship has taught the church the following four lessons:

• **Worship can be full of wonder and awe.**

What place, if any, does planned silence have in your church's worship? Is silence the only way to encourage awe and reverence? Is it the best way? (See also Q&A 16 and 19, pp. 92 and 94.)

Worship centers seek to create an atmosphere of reverence for worship of a holy and transcendent God. Silence and disciplined rituals of gathering are important parts of creating this atmosphere. It is ironic that children's worship is moving in the direction of increased reverence and awe in worship at a time when many congregational worship leaders are doing everything to remove all hints of transcendence and awe.

- **Worship is visual and sensory.**

Children's worship centers are filled with boxes and banners, candles and pictures, color and texture. One specific example of these sensory stimulants is the telling of the Christmas story with the use of the five candles of the Advent wreath and little wooden characters who represent all the characters in the Christmas story. Congregations that have watched the dramatic telling of this story on Christmas morning have been moved not only by the vividness of the story but also by the way their children and grandchildren are almost miraculously drawn into the story. Children today teach us that worship is enriched as we seek to involve all the senses God has given us.

At the same time, we are seeing an increase in sensitivity to visual and artistic dimensions of congregational worship. Artists and banner committees work hard to express carefully the meanings of the seasons of worship through banners, sculptures, and other artistic creations. Drama teams and liturgical dance teams seek to create experiences of worship that give multisensory expression to truths being taught or sung.

- **Worship is centered in story.**

Children's worship centers know the power of story. Children's worship leaders take the biblical stories seriously as stories. That is, the goal in children's worship is not to elicit moral lessons from the biblical story (be kind, don't push, share your cookies) but to draw children into the story, which has its own transforming power. This is a thoroughly Reformed insight into the nature of Scripture and into the way the gospel transforms people. Corresponding to this development in children's worship, many congregational worship leaders are more sensitive today to the variety of ways in which God's Word

Some churches try to create a seeker-comfortable environment by eliminating any explicitly Christian symbols. How do you react to this practice? Are pulpit, font, and table necessary or optional for Christian worship? Is a church without a cross a contradiction in terms?

Are dramatic readings an appropriate way to proclaim Scripture in worship? How about a "dialogue sermon" in which the preacher responds to questions from the congregation? Would showing a video in place of a "live" sermon be acceptable? Why or why not? (See also Q&A 24 and 26, pp. 97-99.)

can be read and communicated (see Heidelberg Catechism Q&A 26).

## • Worship involves the whole body, not just the mind.

What adult is not moved when children in a circle in front of church sing a song with hand motions and body movements that give beautiful physical expression to the words of the song? The psalms have many references to our whole bodies being involved in worship. We kneel in humility before God. We lift our hands in exaltation. *Dance* rather than *dialogue* may be the biblical word to capture the rhythm of Christian worship. (This emphasis upon physicality in worship reminds us of the nature and importance of the sacraments as well. Children may have a purer appreciation of the sacraments themselves and the sacramental nature of worship as a whole than adults, who have overstressed the cognitive dimensions of worship.)

There is a lot we don't know about heaven. But one thing we can be fairly certain of from the psalms and the Revelation of John (Ps. 95:6; Ps. 150; Rev. 19:11) is that our worship will be more physically animated in heaven than it has been in most Christian Reformed congregations here on earth. In heaven we will no doubt wonder how we were able to stay so still in our worship of God. We can reduce the distance between our worship now and our worship in heaven by watching and learning from the physical animation of our children in worship.

Reformed Christians, with a rich view of creation, have core theological reasons to embrace heartily developments that take seriously the multisensory nature of worship and that seek to create a balance in worship between the cerebral and the full-bodied, the abstract and the concrete.

List all the physical acts and gestures you and your fellow worshipers perform in the course of a typical worship service. Can ushering someone into church or hugging a friend be considered a physical act of worship? Should everyone be expected to raise their hands in praise? Is kneeling or making the sign of the cross appropriate? What does your church's *body language* say about how you understand worship?

What do you think *full-bodied* worship would look like? Why is it a rarity in so many churches? Is this a serious problem or simply a cultural curiosity?

## 4. Worship and Evangelism

When God's people worship with pure hearts and in authentic community and when that community is ever renewing its worship, then effective evangelism, that is, the proclamation of the good news of Jesus Christ to those outside the community of faith, will be an organic part of the church's life. Evangelism is not a program tacked onto the church's life; it is an integral part of vital Christian community and worship.

### Three Assumptions About Evangelism

• **Biblical evangelism is communal.**

Biblical evangelism emphasizes the key role of the body of Christ. We come to know Christ in community. To belong to Christ is to belong to those who belong to Christ. The church's goal is to bring unbelievers not just to Jesus Christ but to full life and service in the body of Christ. This principle is important in a very individualistic culture and corrects a fundamentalist tendency to reduce conversion to a single decisional point with little regard for incorporation into a new community.

**Read Romans 12:1-13. In what ways might worship services model both the communal and the personal dimensions of our relationship with Christ?**

• **Biblical evangelism is personal.**

Saying that evangelism is communal does not in any way diminish the importance of each church member's taking seriously his or her calling to personally witness for Christ. Evangelism almost always begins in personal relationships between non-Christians and Christians who are intentional in their efforts to lead a particular person into encounter with Christ.

• **Biblical evangelism is rooted in the heart of God.**

No program of evangelism or tinkering with worship will succeed if people in the church do not have a genuine passion to reach the lost, growing out of God's passion to bring all of his children home. If we do not hurt for those who are perishing, love specific people who are lost, and pray without ceasing for God's Spirit to give new birth, all evangelistic efforts will fall flat.

"Many congregations are quite adept at proclaiming the gospel but very inept at welcoming and assimilating people. Others may be very successful at welcoming and receiving new members but seldom proclaim the gospel. Neither [is] aptly organized to lead people to a public identification with the triune God since both focus on making members, not Christians or disciples. Effective evangelism does both" (Keifert, *Welcoming the Stranger*, p. 5). What is the difference between making members and making disciples?

Many churches today are experiencing frustration in the area of worship and evangelism because they are not putting first things first. If a church does not first have a genuine heart for the lost, then any change in worship designed to make it seem more visitor friendly will be controversial, not to mention ineffective. If a church does not genuinely embody Christian community, then the worship of the church really has little to invite people into. If the worship of a congregation is lifeless and hollow, nonbelievers will not be moved toward God.

When churches do pay attention to first things first, many things about worship and evangelism fall naturally into place. When people have heart, a heart for God in worship and a heart for those who are lost, when the church is a living community of Christ and not just an audience that gathers for a worship performance, and when the church is organically growing in its worship, the church will grow evangelistically.

*Principles Regarding Worship and Evangelism*
Assuming the order of things set forth above, we go on to suggest five principles to guide churches as they think about worship and evangelism.

- **First, communal Christian worship is primarily the activity of believers.**

Do altar calls have a place in Reformed worship? Why or why not? If so, what form should they take?

Sometimes lost in the discussion of worship and evangelism is the fundamental point that Christian worship is first of all the activity of the believing community. Certainly we expect that nonbelievers will be present in Christian worship. And, certainly, although the church does not gather in worship primarily for evangelism, the church must worship in ways that call people to faith and life in Christ. But the fact remains that the church of Jesus Christ that gathers for worship is a believing community that is clearly differentiated from the world.

- **Secondly, we must expect some of Christian worship to seem strange, even unintelligible, to people who do not know Christ.**

Certainly all people are worshipers by nature; the impulse to worship is universal. But Christian worship is the worship of those who have died and risen again to a brand-new life and way of living. In this new community where Christ is head, things are different. Here people are less concerned with finding their life than with losing it for Christ. Here meekness, not muscle, is the mark of greatness. If the church is not radically different from the world, something is radically wrong. To be salt and light in the world implies a marked contrast between the way of life in the world and the way of life in the church. Peter says that Christians are "aliens and strangers in the world" (1 Pet. 2:11). It follows, then, that Christian worship will have its peculiarities.

We disagree with those who suggest that one of the marks of an evangelistically committed church is that people who come to worship there will feel as "at home" in the church as they would in, say, a shopping mall (a recurring image in church-growth circles). The fact is that the church is not a shopping mall, and we should not expect to reduce all distance between the world of the church and the world of the unbeliever. Attempts to erase the differences between the church and the world will harm, not enhance, the church's mission. As Os Guiness has said, "The fastest way to irrelevance is to be obsessed with relevance."

"The worship style that results from the marketing approach to liturgy and evangelism would probably not prompt a child to ask . . . 'Why are we doing this?' . . . The question would not be asked because there is nothing 'odd' about such liturgies. They are not out of step with the world and therefore they cannot present a real alternative to the world's claims" (Senn, *The Witness of the Worshiping Community*, p. 20). To what extent, if any, does effective evangelism depend on being "odd"?

Authorities on worship as varied as Marva J. Dawn (*Reaching Out Without Dumbing Down*) and Sally Morgenthaler (*Worship Evangelism: Inviting Unbelievers into the Presence of God*), whose book titles indicate how differently they approach worship, nevertheless strongly agree with Guiness's point. Which aspects of your church's worship might seem strange and irrelevant to an unchurched visitor? Why? How can these aspects be more inviting without "dumbing down"?

## • Third, churches must seek to be as visitor friendly and seeker friendly as possible.

"Ritual . . . provides the sense of cover that allows most people to feel safe enough to participate in expressions of religious value. Despite how things may seem when a visitor comes to church for the first time, ritual can in fact be most hospitable to the congregational stranger" (Keifert, *Welcoming the Stranger,* p. 110). What personal experiences would lead you to agree or disagree with Keifert?

Churches must eliminate all unnecessary barriers to communication with visitors and seekers. The key word here is *unnecessary*. As we saw in the second principle on page 71, there is an irreducible distance or chasm between the church and the world that only the Holy Spirit can bridge. Below we address those barriers between the church and nonbelievers that are simply a matter of careless communication and that can be reduced or removed. Often the church, in its worship, through acts of omission or commission, unnecessarily erects barriers between itself and the seeker.

Consider some of the simple things a church can do to eliminate barriers:

• Avoid or explain in-house references. Not everyone knows what *NIV* (New International Version) or *CRC* (Christian Reformed Church) or *CRWRC* (Christian Reformed World Relief Committee) means.

• Clarify what is happening in worship. Brief explanations at critical points in worship can help all worshipers, not just visitors and seekers, understand what is happening, and they need not detract from the flow of worship.

• Produce the church bulletin with the visitor and seeker in mind. Replace the liturgical terms *salutation* with *God's greeting* and *benediction* with *God's blessing.* Be specific about where children meet for children's worship.

• Explicitly express to visitors and seekers your joy that they are with you in worship. (Do this only if it's true. The test, of course, is what visitors experience after worship in terms of greeting and fellowship and after Sunday in terms of community.)

- Design the content of services with visitors and seekers in mind. The prayers, the sermon, the introductions to songs must be sensitive to the full spiritual range of people who are present.

- **Fourth, changes in worship should be organic, from the inside out, not imposed, from the outside in.**

We have argued that the best changes in worship, especially in music, are changes that proceed from a strong *centeredness* and changes that proceed carefully, integratively, and pastorally. Worship changes that violate these principles in the name of evangelism and the hope of reaching people who are not yet present in worship services do violence to the church's worship, will be destructive of the church community, and will fail to attract the very people the church wants to attract.

For example, instead of asking what music is needed to attract a nameless, faceless person who has not yet even come to worship, it would be more helpful to ask what music will enable all members who are already present to worship God more fully. In nearly every congregation there are children and young people, persons who have joined from other church backgrounds, and people who have joined through conversion. In every congregation people are already present who challenge the church to think creatively about changes in worship. As we change worship to connect with them, we also will be changing worship in ways that will connect more effectively with seekers.

Think about a typical service in your church. How many of these ideas have been implemented? Which things do you think your church does best? Which areas could stand improvement? What other ideas could you add to the list?

See Q&A 1-9, pages 80-88.

"If the faith is truly to be learned, it must be taught. If singing the faith is crucial (and we know it is), then it too must be taught. . . . Vigorous and informed singing is not simply frill. It is a fundamental way of rejoicing, praying, learning, worshiping, and proclaiming the gospel" (Best, *Music Through the Eyes of Faith*, p. 201). How can members and seekers alike find the music in your worship more *crucial*, *vigorous*, and *informed*?

This principle of changing from the inside out addresses the very common practice today of borrowing from or copying worship practices that other churches are using. In an age when many churches market themselves as models to be imitated and in an age when many of our church members worship in other churches and experience new things in worship, local churches are constantly bombarded with new things to try in worship.

An old maxim holds that the way we worship shapes what we believe. Can we borrow worship styles and practices from other Christian traditions and still remain Reformed? How?

Certainly churches learn from one another. Each church has particular strengths, and other churches can learn from those strengths. The body of Christ has ears and hands and feet, and we need all those parts to make the body whole. The issue is not whether there should be giving and receiving, a cross-fertilization of ideas and experiences, among churches. The issue is how a local church should incorporate into its own church community practices that another church is using. The point here is that churches must do so from the inside out—carefully, integratively, and pastorally.

Identify things that make your church unique. Do any of these relate to the way you worship? Are there some worship practices that would "never go over" in your church? Why?

One of the biggest church leadership conferences in North America right now is the conference at Willow Creek Community Church near Chicago. Pastor Bill Hybels uses the image of a thumbprint to emphasize the importance of churches changing from within. Each person has a unique thumbprint. So does each church. Each church is unique in terms of place, time, congregation, community, history, resources, and so forth. An idea cannot be applied in exactly the same way in any two churches. An idea or a principle has to be digested by a church and applied in ways that are appropriate for that particular church. There is no "one size fits all" when it comes to the ministry and worship of the church.

- **Finally, worship leaders must remember that there is a little lostness in all of us.**

It is easy for pastors and worship leaders to draw a firm line between believers and nonbelievers and to assume that all members of the church are believers. As worship leaders, we would do well to remind ourselves of Jesus' parable of the wheat and the weeds (Matt. 13:24-30), where Jesus teaches that believers and nonbelievers are not so easily separated. The asterisk by a person's name in the church directory indicating that person's church membership does not guarantee that that name is written in the Book of Life. Second, even as true believers we must remind ourselves that the most mature saint in the church needs to be called home, called to faith, and called anew to the cross. The gospel call to faith and commitment is a call that Christians must hear and say yes to again and again.

What forms might this call to faith and commitment take? Is the sermon the only place it can be given?

Therefore pastors and worship leaders should not feel that parts of worship that are specifically geared to the nonbeliever have no relevance or positive spiritual value for believers. Just as nonbelievers can be blessed as they overhear the encounter between God and his people, so believers can be blessed as they hear the worship leader call nonbelievers to faith and commitment.

---

### REFORMED WORSHIP

---

Finally, we address the question of *Reformed* worship. Is there such a thing as Reformed worship? Or is there only Christian worship? What are the "nonnegotiables" of Reformed worship that synod mandated its committee to identify? What is the Reformed character of worship?

Does refusal to insist on *nonnegotiables* make everything negotiable? If so, is this a problem? What do you think are the most effective ways to cultivate the gifts of the Reformed tradition? (See also Q&A 14, pp. 90-91.)

Our committee seriously wrestled with these important questions. We concluded that it was not particularly helpful to talk about the non-negotiables of Reformed worship as though Reformed worship were something totally distinct from (and superior to) Christian worship and something that we must feverishly defend and protect lest it be forever lost. Rather, we concluded that it was more helpful and honest to talk about *Christian* worship and then to acknowledge that, like every other worship tradition, the Reformed worship tradition has both received gifts from and given gifts to Christian worship and that what it has given has arisen out of what it has first received. In that spirit we note some of the gifts to Christian worship that the Reformed tradition has made over the centuries and encourage the continued cultivation of these gifts. Most of these gifts noted below have already been explored in our preceding theological reflection.

With gratitude to God we note the following eight gifts as some of the particular gifts that the Reformed tradition has made to Christian worship:

- A redemptive-historical perspective on worship (a) that takes seriously the rich communion of relationships in worship—from the relationships within the holy Trinity, to the relationships between God and his people, to the relationships among God's people (here and now and throughout history—from Abraham to the saints around the throne) and (b) that takes seriously the intimate connection between service and love of God and service and love of neighbor and the need for integrity of these two. Also implicit in this rich redemptive-historical perspective is an understanding of the relationship of church and kingdom that keeps Christian worship always directed out beyond itself into service in every dimension of life in God's world.

- A fully trinitiarian emphasis in worship that seeks balanced attention to God the Father, God the Son, and God the Holy Spirit.

- An understanding that preaching is proclamation of the Word of God that results in a Spirit-charged encounter with God, not mere lecture or instruction. In this connection, it is significant that in Reformed worship the Holy Spirit is traditionally invoked not only in the context of the sacraments but also in the context of the reading and preaching of the Word (the prayer for illumination).

- An emphasis upon doctrinal preaching (most clearly exemplified by catechism preaching).

- Calvin's sacramental theology that emphasizes the real presence of Christ in the sacraments (over against a view of the sacraments as mere symbols).

- A particular emphasis upon the acts of worship that arise out of a view of worship as true encounter with God. These include the salutation, the declaration of pardon, the prayer for illumination, and the benediction.

- A conviction that congregational singing is at the heart of worship music, integrated into every part of worship, and a corresponding caution that congregational singing should not be minimized and/or swallowed up by other forms of worship music.

How can doctrinal preaching avoid becoming mere lecture or instruction? How, or to what extent, can catechism preaching address both seekers and mature believers?

For a long time most Reformed churches opposed using choirs in worship; some still do. If congregational singing is primary, what legitimate role(s) does a choir have? Does "special music" have any place in worship services? If so, what is it? (See also Q&A 7, 8, and 16, pp. 86-87 and 92.)

There are many different ways of singing the psalms, including metrical settings, psalm chants, and responsorial singing. How can your church musicians be encouraged to investigate and demonstrate examples of these various ways?

What other gifts, if any, do you think this list should have included? What gifts from other traditions might contribute to authentic Reformed worship?

- A strong appreciation of the Old Testament in general and of psalm singing in particular as part of public worship. (Much of the Reformed emphasis upon the psalms and the Old Testament is related to the redemptive-historical theology set forth above.)

Although churches in the Reformed tradition may not be the only churches that have appreciated these elements of worship, we see these as eight gifts that Reformed worship has given to worship in the Christian church. We also see them as gifts that we should continue to emphasize and cultivate in the Christian Reformed Church.

# AQuestions and
# Answers

In this section our goal is to apply our cultural analysis from Section One and our theological reflection from Section Two to *specific issues* in Christian worship today. This is a difficult task for at least two reasons. First, it's possible to agree on certain cultural analyses and theological principles but to disagree on how they apply to a specific matter of worship. Second, each congregation is unique and must take into account its own particular situation as it relates these insights to its worship. Each congregation is unique in many ways: its history, its geographical and demographic context, its members and the particular gifts they possess, its pastor, its specific goals. While certain biblical-theological principles are the same in every congregation, how those principles apply will vary greatly from situation to situation.

The format we are using is a question-and-answer format. Although we cannot deal with all the issues, we have tried to select real questions that congregations are struggling with today. We realize that some of the questions we pose may be quickly dated.

We are less concerned that readers agree with every answer we give and more concerned that readers notice two things:

- first, how the cultural analyses and theological reflections of the previous two sections inform the way we address these difficult questions;

- second, how discernment and wisdom are as important as expertise in culture and worship when it comes to dealing with many of the controversial matters in worship today.

We have divided the questions into two broad categories: general issues and particular parts of the liturgy.

---

**GENERAL ISSUES**

---

**1. We have been trying to change some things in our worship service, but many people in our church dismiss everything we want to do as "turning worship into entertainment." Sometimes I see what they mean, but other times it just seems like a discussion stopper. Help!**

The problem with the word *entertainment* is that five different people who use it mean five different things by it. Some would call *entertainment* whatever aims at people's feelings. That's too simplistic, since all worship should touch us at the feeling level. And we agree that just giving something a label or epithet doesn't get us anywhere. People must explain what they mean when they use terms like *entertainment*.

Having said that, we also agree that entertainment does refer to tendencies in worship today that we would regard as troubling. We would share your fellow church members' concern about worship services becoming entertainment when worship increasingly displays the following three tendencies:

- Worship services that focus upon the feeling response of the worshiper to the exclusion of other important responses (for example, the response of the intellect and the will).

In a therapeutic culture, where my felt needs and my self-fulfillment are all-important, it is easy for the sole criterion of worship to be how worship makes me feel. Worship becomes very self-centered, even infantile, concerned only with what worship does for me. Self-gratification becomes the unacknowledged purpose of worship.

At the risk of sounding harsh, we would say that if someone lives in a town with twenty-five churches and asserts that none of them is good enough to meet his or her spiritual needs, that person is saying more about him- or herself than about those churches. And what that person is criticizing probably involves a misunderstanding of what worship is supposed to *do* for the worshiper and an excessive concern with how worship makes a person feel.

- Worship services that are easy.

A current tendency in worship is to make worship easy—easy to move into, easy to move out of. The worshiper can just sit back and watch. Worship leaders (musicians, pastors, and liturgists) take responsibility for the worship experience. They perform for the "audience." Few demands are put on the worshiper.

As Calvin M. Johansson says, the fundamental posture of worship is not "sitting back"; it is "leaning forward" (*Music and Ministry*). Worship is active, not passive. And worship both creates and relieves tension. Worship disturbs and comforts. In worship we die and rise with Christ. Genuine worship is hard spiritual work.

Of course, one must distinguish here between Christian worship and an evangelistic event. Easy access may be appropriate for services that are planned as evangelistic events, but not for services planned as Christian worship.

• Worship services that are excessive.

The secular entertainment model thrives on making the entertainment experience (and the entertainer) seem larger than life. Not every solo (or organ accompaniment) must bring us to a new level of ecstasy. To worship God, we should not need million-dollar smiles from attractive model-like worship leaders, and we must absolutely renounce strategies that deliberately seek to cultivate a celebrity-like aura around a church's senior pastor. When every worship service must be a ten on a scale of one to ten in terms of impact on the worshiper, worship leaders soon get exhausted, and worshipers feel like Johnny who ate all the candy—bloated and empty at the same time. An increasingly *soloistic* and celebrity-oriented approach to worship and music is leaving less and less room in worship for the simple, unadorned song of God's people.

This is not a defense of mediocrity and laziness in worship leadership. Certainly the worship services of some churches must be called what they are: boring. But in an entertainment culture, the charge of "boring" is overused and too often employs a standard for evaluating worship that comes more from Hollywood than from the Sermon on the Mount. Blessed are the meek. Blessed are churches that can sing and worship with great simplicity and say, "It was good to have been here."

**2. But all three of the things you mention describe the people we're trying to reach. We may not like it, but the fact is that people in our culture are self-absorbed, they demand instant gratification, and they are addicted to overstimulation. How else are we going to reach these people except to move worship in precisely the direction you call entertainment?**

Certainly we must realize that these are the culturally induced spiritual handicaps that people bring to worship. And our challenge as worship leaders is to create worship that communicates to and engages people who have these handicaps. Unfortunately, there is a very fine line between engaging these people and capitulating to their handicaps. We must help each other walk that line. For example, it's fine to shorten a scripture reading from fifty-three verses to thirteen verses out of sensitivity to the attention span of the contemporary worshiper, but to quit reading Scripture in worship because the worshiper thinks Scripture reading is boring is capitulation, not sensitivity.

Our goal as worship leaders is to exercise wisdom and discernment *that flow out of a strong faith in the power of the gospel.* We must believe that when worship is directed to God through Jesus Christ and in the power of the Holy Spirit and when worship is from the heart, done in authentic Christian community, and is ever renewing and being renewed by the Spirit, then God will bless that worship.

**3. Our congregation is hopelessly divided on worship style. We are seriously thinking about going to two morning services—one contemporary and one traditional. Any advice?**

Yes. Talk to congregations that have made this move. Some congregations have done it with great blessing, especially where there were unique things about their outreach mission that drove the decision. However, many congregations have experienced two alternative worship services as trading the demons they did know for the demons they didn't know.

Here are five things to consider:

- If the congregation still has a well-attended evening service, the struggle between these two worship styles simply shifts to the evening service.

- A congregation must seriously weigh its motivation for having alternative worship services. If the primary motivation is to resolve conflict, it probably will not succeed. The conflict probably will only intensify. The motivation should be positive and should flow from the church's mission and purpose.

- Each group is impoverished by not having elements from the worship of the other. Each of these two worship styles has strengths, and the best worship incorporates the strengths of both.

- A church must carefully count the cost of two alternative services in terms of additional resources demanded by two different services. Those resources include more time spent by pastors, musicans, dramatists, and liturgists in planning entirely different services.

- Though some churches (particularly Roman Catholic churches) have very different worship styles within the same congregation and maintain a clear sense of identity, most Christian Reformed churches are so centrally defined by their style of worship that the introduction of two styles of worship into one congregation essentially creates two congregations.

You might reassess just how hopeless your situation is. We are aware of a congregation in your church's situation that seriously considered, but rejected, the alternative-services approach. Instead it recommitted itself to worship that incorporated the best of both traditional and contemporary worship. In its mission statement the congregation committed itself to balance in worship, describing balanced worship as worship that is in these words:

*sensitive to the* seeker *as well as the long-time worshiper,*
*warm and personal as well as ordered and dignified,*
*flexible and varied as well as predictable and stable.*

Hard work toward that kind of balance has paid off in terms of a congregation that is once again united in its worship.

Again, in some situations, two services may be the best solution. We would recommend caution and extensive conversation with churches where alternative services have been positive and with churches where they have been negative.

**4. Why do people get so bothered when we use taped background music to accompany our soloists? Our church doesn't have very good piano players. It seems like a good alternative.**

This question raises a broader issue: the use of spiritual gifts. One can oppose taped background music because it sounds contrived or because it plays into the "bigger than life" syndrome we discussed in Question 1. Or one can support taped background music because it gives the soloist flawless accompaniment and adds emotional impact to the solo. But those arguments are peripheral to a much larger issue, namely, what do we believe about spiritual gifts?

Healthy worship renewal takes seriously the spiritual gifts God has given his people for use in worship. If we believe that God has given spiritual gifts for leadership in worship, that suggests the following principle or guideline regarding electronic substitutes in worship: we will seek to discover, cultivate, and use the gifts of God's people who are present in worship rather than relying on electronic substitutes. Churches that are following this principle are discovering gifts they never realized were present in their congregations. It's hard work, but it will pay off in the end.

(We must recognize that the line between these two choices is fuzzier than it might first appear. How should we categorize the person playing the synthesizer with preprogrammed background chords?)

**5. As we use a greater variety of songs in our worship, some of the music types in our church say that a service must have musical integrity. By that they mean we should do only one type of music in a given service. So if we want to do gospel music, the whole service should be gospel. But we should not sing contemporary and gospel and traditional in the same service. What about that?**

It's good to ask the question of integrity: What is the thread that holds the service together? What gives it unity? One way to answer that question as it relates to music is to say, as you suggest in your question, that all the music of a particular service should be of the same musical genre (gospel, traditional, praise and worship). Congregations tend to go this route when they are quite unfamiliar with a new genre of music. It seems too dissonant and jerky to move from "Precious Lord, Take My Hand" to "Jerusalem the Golden."

But when a congregation becomes more comfortable with new songs, it moves more easily between genres of music. At that point it is helpful to see an alternative for defining integrity of a service. Instead of defining the integrity of a service by musical genre, we suggest you define the integrity (unity, cohesiveness) in terms of the theme of a particular service (thematically, both "Precious Lord, Take My Hand" and "Jerusalem the Golden" fit a service dealing with the comfort of Christ's return).

**6. I'm a Hispanic member of the Christian Reformed Church and worship in a Spanish-speaking congregation. Our worship services seem very different from worship services in some of the large, established Christian Reformed churches I've visited. Whose worship is this report dealing with? Does this report apply to our congregation's worship?**

Yes, it does. At the level of style, worship services may seem very different from each other. But the underlying structure should still be the same. In this report we have argued for a basic structure to worship. But within that structure are tremendous freedom and variety. You are right to point out the enormous variety of worship styles just within the Christian Reformed Church, not to mention the entire Christian church. We have tried to address worship not at the level of one particular style or cultural orientation but at the level of the enduring structure of worship that crosses cultural lines. This concept of *freedom within structure* is an exciting concept for churches from different cultural backgrounds that are seeking to affirm their unity with one another in Christ.

**7. Our church is considering the formation of a worship team, a team of four to eight people who will lead some of the singing in worship. Is this a good idea?**

Worship teams can be very helpful in worship, particularly when you are trying to teach the congregation new songs. Confident leadership from the worship team gives the congregation guidance and confidence.

Some churches that have a big band and a worship team that lead an extended set of songs at the beginning of the service have discovered that the congregation is not singing or not singing very well. Several factors may be at work here:

• The congregation includes many unchurched people who are not used to singing.

• The volume of the accompaniment (often a band) and singers (usually miked) is so overpowering that people can't hear themselves sing, and so they quit singing.

• The singing goes on too long, and people get tired and quit.

A good test of congregational singing is what happens when the accompaniment and leadership drop out. The congregation, not the leaders, should be carrying the congregational song. Most worship teams that we are familiar with are sensitive to these concerns and see themselves not as performers but as leaders of the congregation.

**8. Our congregation's choir is on the rocks. We just can't get enough people to commit themselves to the time it takes to practice. What should we do?**

You are not alone. Many churches in your situation are going to seasonal choirs to give people the option of shorter commitments. For example, you might have an Advent choir for four weeks, a Lenten/Easter choir for six weeks, a men's chorus for three weeks, a women's chorus for three weeks. Each choir probably will have the same core of people, but another group of people in the church will probably be willing to make more limited commitments to one or two such choirs.

Many churches are being forced to rethink the purpose of the choir. Is it to give accomplished performances of difficult, sophisticated music, or is it to lead the congregation in worship? As congregations are seeking greater diversity in their worship, many churches are coming to see the role of the choir less as performance and more as leader of the congregation. We think that is the right direction, especially for churches with limited resources in this area.

In this regard it is significant that church choirs and worship teams are both moving the church in the same direction—away from the performance of a few to the singing of the congregation as a whole.

**9. I think we care more about preserving our own style of worship than we do about reaching unbelievers. Isn't it possible to be too concerned with little things in Christian worship and not concerned enough about people who might be there searching for Christ?**

You have put your finger on a great problem in many discussions of Christian worship. Let's be honest. Many of us don't care much about nonbelievers. We're more concerned with our own comfort zones in worship than with people going to hell.

In this regard, we suggest you sensitively give this test to someone who truly doesn't seem to care about unbelievers. Or imagine that you have a daughter who marries an unbeliever. Of course we hope and pray that never happens. But it does happen all the time. Your son-in-law, the father of your grandchildren, never comes to church. But now, for some reason, he has started coming. How do you see worship as you view it through the eyes of your son-in-law? Are there unnecessary obstacles and barriers in worship?

The point of the test is this: if we loved the stranger, the one lost sheep, as much as we love our own families, no doubt we would look at some things in worship differently. As we say in the worship and evangelism section [Section Two, pp. 69-75], there is no substitute for heartfelt love for the unbeliever.

The test above cuts both ways. You don't want unnecessary barriers for your son-in-law. But you also don't want anything less than authentic Christian worship. You've gained little if the son-in-law comes to church but finds there something other than authentic worship of God the Father through Jesus Christ in the power of the Spirit.

Nevertheless, your point is exactly right. We must first love the unbeliever as we love our own children. And then we must make decisions about Christian worship.

### 10. What's a seeker service?

It's important to distinguish between *seeker-driven* and *seeker-sensitive* worship services. Seeker-sensitive worship simply refers to worship services that are friendly and intelligible to the outsider. Worship planners and leaders should always be striving to make worship seeker sensitive. It's important to remind ourselves that the widespread decline in biblical-theological literacy in effect makes seekers out of many of the church's own members.

The seeker-driven service goes one step further and refers more to an evangelistic strategy than to a worship service. The seeker-driven service focuses on the person the church wants to reach and designs every part of the service in light of that person's perceptions, experiences, and needs. Designers of seeker-driven services are unapologetic in making the audience and the goal of communicating the gospel to that audience the shaping forces of the service and don't concern themselves much with historic patterns of worship. A seeker-driven service is not intended to be a substitute for Christian worship and is usually offered in addition to a more traditional worship service.

More resources on the seeker-driven service are available from Willow Creek Association, a ministry arm of Willow Creek Community Church (see Additional Resources for Study and Planning, p. 106).

**11. People in our church come back from conferences and talk about worship for baby boomers and worship for baby busters. I'm not convinced. Did Paul have a buster church?**

No, but Paul was very aware of his specific audience. Books have been written on Paul's sermons in the book of Acts specifically analyzing how carefully he crafted each sermon to connect with the specific audience to whom he was preaching. At one level our talk today about worship for boomers or busters is only a new version of the time-tested mission principle that we must establish a point of contact with those to whom we minister. Pastors and worship leaders must work hard to understand different segments of the church and society to whom they seek to minister.

As a committee, we do have questions about the wisdom of defining a congregation's mission solely in terms of a single generation. One of the wonderful things about the church throughout its history has been its multigenerational character. We see great wisdom in keeping the church that way and not overspecializing in worship. In fact, though we support the developments in children's worship and believe that younger children benefit greatly from a combination of worship with the whole congregation and children's worship, we also feel strongly that children must become fully integrated into the worship of the whole congregation as soon as possible. Worship leaders must take children into account in planning worship. But we must also realize that worship has a positive impact on children even though they may not fully comprehend everything that is going on. In defending the idea that children should be part of worship at young ages, one church leader even said, "Some of my greatest childhood memories of church are falling asleep during the sermon snuggled up against my mom."

**12. We're from a small rural congregation. When we go to worship conferences and see what different churches are doing, we just get depressed because we don't have the resources—money and people—that many other churches have. Any suggestions?**

Yes, and they apply to virtually every church. Virtually every church must fight the tendency to compare itself negatively to churches that have many more resources for worship. God does not call a church to be like some other church. God calls a church to do the very best with the resources God has given it. Many churches look silly as they seek to be something they are not. Thank God for what your church has and build upon it; don't waste your time pining about what some other church has that you don't have.

**13. Why don't we let the Spirit lead more in worship? Why does everything need to be so planned out all the time?**

We need to be sensitive to the Holy Spirit in each worship service. And we must be willing to follow where the Spirit leads. But we shouldn't link the Holy Spirit with less planning or less formality. The Holy Spirit can be powerfully present in a very highly structured, liturgical service and can be absent in a service with little structure. Beyond style and level of formality, the question always before us is this: Does this act of worship bring praise to God through Jesus Christ in the Holy Spirit? The answer to that question can be yes in many different styles of worship.

**14. Aren't there certain basic elements that must be in a worship service for it even to be a worship service—like the confession of sin, a sermon, and an offering?**

A good question, but we prefer to get at this from a little different angle. Instead of asking what the mandatory elements of a worship service are, we prefer to ask a couple of other questions:

- What happens when people worship God?

- What are the constants, the universals, the enduring components to worship that can be observed as we *watch* God's people worship over the continents and centuries?

This descriptive rather than prescriptive approach avoids legalistic wranglings about whether a particular worship service was *true worship* because of some liturgical variation in that service and still addresses the important concern we sense in the question, namely, are there certain enduring components to worship that we as a worshiping community ignore at our own peril? The answer to the latter question is yes. Confession of sin, affirmation of faith in the triune God, proclamation of God's Word, responding in thanksgiving through presentation of offerings—these are enduring components of Christian worship that should be part of every worship service and absent only by exception and with strong rationale.

We fear that the pendulum often swings wildly from one extreme to the other. One extreme is a wooden uniformity that allows for no local freedom and creativity. The other extreme is local creativity that totally cuts itself off from the mainstream of Christian worship. We think the concept of *freedom within structure* that we've argued for in this report avoids the problems of both extremes.

A particular example of this swinging pendulum is evident in the use of sacramental forms. One extreme is to allow for no flexibility in how the liturgical forms for the sacraments are used in a particular worship service. The other extreme is for a local congregation simply to throw out the forms and do whatever it pleases. Churches that do so need to be reminded that the liturgy of holy communion does not belong to one local congregation; it belongs to the whole church. Again, we hope that the concept of freedom within structure that we have set forth in this report will restrain the wild swings of the pendulum from total inflexibility to total flexibility.

**15. As a worship leader I have noticed that conferences on worship seem to ignore preaching and conferences on preaching seem to ignore worship. Conferences on worship seem to be poorly attended by pastors. Aren't preaching and worship integrally related?**

Yes. In this report we have purposely avoided talking about preaching and worship as though they were two separate things. Preaching is an integral part of worship, and worship is the vital context of preaching. Neither can be separated from the other. We are encouraged by increasing emphasis in seminaries on all the dimensions of public worship, including preaching and the sacraments. Seminaries that hope to equip future pastors need professors of worship as well as professors of preaching.

**16. Some people in our church think applause is wrong because it praises the performer instead of praising God. What's so bad about doing both?**

It depends. Here is one of those issues that require great doses of wisdom and common sense. We cannot come up with rules for applause. Consider the following examples of where applause might be a spontaneous and totally appropriate way for a congregation to express its joy or appreciation or love:

- the recognition of a couple who have been married fifty years,

- the recognition of the members of the second-grade church school class who have been presented their Bibles,

- the announcement that a mother who has been in the hospital for three months has safely delivered triplets,

- the announcement that a beloved pastor has declined a call.

Spontaneous applause that expresses joy and thanksgiving is not alien to the spirit and purpose of worship.

Applause becomes more problematic when, in essence, it is something programmed. To give applause every time someone sings a solo in church, regardless of whether the solo moved you or not, quickly becomes programmed applause. Such applause is also arbitrary. Why applaud soloists only? Why not applaud a great sermon or a great offertory by the organist?

Applause is one way in our culture that we express joy, appreciation, honor, and thanksgiving. ("Amen" is a form of *verbal applause* that serves the same function in some churches.) The challenge is to keep applause from being predictable and, in fact, cut off from genuine feelings of joy, appreciation, honor, and thanksgiving. When applause genuinely expresses those feelings in the context of our relationship with one another in Christ, let it happen.

**17. What is the place of humor in worship?**

Laughter is one of God's great gifts. People in strong community know how to cry together and laugh together. So much of the light that God's Word sheds on life leads us to laugh—at ourselves and with others who laugh at themselves. Of course, we are not suggesting that laughter is the goal of worship. We are not advocating a spot in the liturgy called "joke of the week." But there is nothing unspiritual or even unworshipful about the community of God's people laughing together. The opposite could probably be argued: wholesome laughter is in fact a mark of healthy Christian community.

**18. It seems that we laugh more in church than we used to, but it also seems that we cry more in church. What's going on here?**

It's probably fair to say that in the past Christians (at least Christian Reformed Christians) have tried to separate their worship from their personal pain and brokenness. That is, they left their problems at home when they came to worship. Both cultural factors (see "We hurt," pp. 31-34) and other influences on worship (particularly the charismatic influence) have changed that for more and more people. Today we tend to take our brokenness with us to church and offer it up as part of the broken self that worships.

For the most part, this is a positive development. The psalms are filled with examples of worship in the middle of brokenness, not worship walled off from brokenness. How wonderful that Christians can share the burdens they have with child raising, or mental illness, or alcoholism, or marital strife and can do so in the context of worship and community in such a way that all members of the body are strengthened and blessed.

Many churches actually design services around the expression of such brokenness. Services of lament focus upon our collective brokenness. Services of healing and prayer offer people the opportunity to bring their brokenness to the Christian community and receive prayer and healing mercy from God.

Often worship leaders must be sensitive to the presence of children in worship as they decide how to deal with certain crises. For example, if a congregation is shaken by the attempted suicide of one of its young people, there is a way to worship that fully takes into account our pain and brokenness and still respects the rights of parents to decide how best to deal with such sensitive issues with their own young children. Obviously, pastors must be very sensitive to the privacy rights of people and make the personal brokenness of a member or members a matter of public worship only when the member or members agree and when doing so will be edifying and upbuilding for the whole body.

### 19. What is the role of silence in worship?

Silence can be very meaningful in worship. The Old Testament psalmists and prophets often called the people to be silent so they could hear God speaking. A time of silence for individual confession of sin, silence during the passing of the elements of communion, leaving the sanctuary in silence after a Good Friday service—these are examples of silence as a meaningful and dramatic part of worship.

It's important to think through these things in planning the service. It's also important, at first anyway, to make clear to the congregation the purpose and goal of a particular time of silence. In North American culture we are addicted to noise. We tend to be very uncomfortable with silence. In order for silence in worship to be meaningful and not distracting, we must be explicit and clear. A simple statement will do: "During the passing of the cup, we meditate in silence upon the love of Christ for us."

### 20. I'm not a stick-in-the-mud when it comes to innovations in worship, but I tire of coming to church each Sunday and wondering what is going to happen. I like surprises on my birthday, not when I go to church.

You put your finger on a problem in many churches today. People have a need for innovation and freshness and vitality in worship. They also have a need for stability and predictability. Worship leaders must remember both of these needs as they plan worship. Often churches that have experienced *innovation burnout* discipline themselves by some of the following guidelines:

• Don't change something in worship for just one week.

If it's worth doing once, it should be worth doing with some regularity so that people can get used to it. For example, it's fine to experiment with more meaningful ways to celebrate communion. But don't change every time. Try something and stick with it for a while.

- Limit yourself to a certain number of new songs.

Rather than singing a new song three times over a six-week period and then moving on to another new song and then to yet another, begin the year with a specific list of songs and close the list to new songs for that year. Each year, once a year, open the list and consider adding some new songs. This practice keeps churches from going through new songs like peppermints, and disciplines worship planners to be thoughtful about what songs they are using in worship.

- Take the "five small steps forward" approach.

Avoid the violence (and folly) of the "one giant step forward, three steps backward, one small step forward" approach, which in the end leaves a congregation one step behind where it was when it began making changes.

Change is difficult for all of us. Be wise, and change can be meaningful and significant.

---

| **PARTICULAR PARTS OF THE LITURGY** |

**21. Our church has just started mutual greetings, where we turn to greet each other early in the worship service. Some people call it a distraction. They say they came to worship God, not to greet Joe. Is a time of greeting one another so bad?**

No. We worship as the body of Christ. A time of greeting one another, welcoming visitors, interacting between adults and children can only enrich worship that is the worship of the body of Christ.

Sometimes people oppose the exchange of mutual greetings because it seems to be part of a broader package of changes, the unspoken goal of which seems to be to remove all vestiges of reverence and dignity from worship. That, of course, is a different matter. But on the narrow question of mutual greetings, our hunch is that when the early church "devoted themselves to the apostles' teaching and to the fellowship, to the breaking of bread and to prayer" (Acts 2:42), Joe got not only greetings but also hugs of joy and sorrow.

**22. Our previous pastor always prayed the prayer of confession and the congregational prayer spontaneously. Our current pastor always has these prayers fully written out ahead of time. Which is the better way to do it?**

God wants prayers that are from the heart. Both spontaneous prayers and written prayers can be equally genuine and edifying. Both can also be heartless. The danger of using prayers written out ahead of time is that they may sound as if they are being read, not prayed. The danger of spontaneous prayers is that they can easily become mindlessly repetitious week after week. Our hunch is that churches where prayer is a powerful part of the worship service probably have some combination of both prepared and spontaneous prayers.

**23. Who is allowed to do the congregational prayer?**

This question is part of the broader question of unordained leadership in worship. Traditionally, we have considered as *official acts of ministry* (those acts of ministry reserved for ordained clergy) these four parts of worship:

- the salutation,
- the benediction,
- the sermon,
- and the administration of the sacraments.

Synod is currently studying the concept of official acts of ministry. It seems safe to say that the general direction is away from the question who is *allowed* to lead in worship? to the question who is *gifted* to lead in worship?

Even traditionally the congregational prayer has never been considered an official act of ministry that can be performed only by clergy. Some churches expand the number of those who lead in this prayer to include elders in addition to the pastor. The biblical principle here is to use people who have gifts to lead in this important part of worship. In addition, elders are called to spiritual leadership and prayer. Those who lead the prayers of the people should be spiritually mature, fervent, discerning as to the needs of the congregation and the world, thoroughly familiar with the congregation, and spiritually respected by the congregation.

**24. We hear of a lot of churches that are using minidramas in their worship services. Where does this practice come from? Should we be doing it?**

Willow Creek Community Church in suburban Chicago has popularized the use of minidramas in worship services. The Willow Creek Association offers mountains of resources for congregations trying to do minidramas for worship. Typically, minidramas, like good sermon introductions, serve to uncover a need that the gospel addresses.

Congregations must do what God has called and gifted them to do. We have already referred to Pastor Bill Hybels's concept of the congregational thumbprint. As each congregation has a unique thumbprint, so also each congregation has unique gifts and opportunities for ministry. If your congregation has the gifts to carry on this particular kind of ministry, that's great. If not, that's fine too.

As congregations experiment with these things, it's important that they keep straight what they are doing. These various forms of worship should all be ways of more effectively communicating, hearing, and responding to God's Word. In this regard it's also helpful to expand our understanding of drama in worship. Baptism and communion are dramas. The reading of Scripture, if not a drama in itself, should be dramatic. The history of salvation is a drama. The liturgical church year is a drama built around the life of Christ. Each Christmas and Good Friday and Easter and Ascension Day and Pentecost we reenact the drama. One of the contributions of minidramas to Christian worship has been to open our eyes to many dramatic features of Christian worship and to strengthen the dramatic power of all worship.

**25. Our pastor talks about Scripture readings from the "common lectionary." What is the lectionary anyway?**

The *Revised Common Lectionary* is a three-year schedule of Scripture readings to be used each Sunday in worship. Each Sunday has a reading from the Old Testament, the Gospels, and the Epistles. A psalm is also listed for each Sunday.

This question leads to the larger question of how ministers and worship leaders decide upon texts for preaching. Christian Reformed churches already have one *lectionary* in place: the Heidelberg

Catechism. Regular preaching of the catechism gives doctrinal balance and breadth to the preaching ministry of the church in the same way that lectionary preaching seeks to give balance and breadth in terms of biblical material.

Another method of text selection is the use of a particular book of the Bible. A pastor can preach a series of sermons on the book of Romans that runs for two weeks or two years. This method of text selection has the advantage of giving listeners in-depth insight into one particular book of the Bible.

All three of these methods of text selection are helpful for worship-planning committees and musicians, who need to know the texts and themes of worship services far in advance for planning purposes. They also guard against the imbalances in preaching that can result when the pastor alone chooses every preaching text. Ideally, a combination of the selection methods above will enable the church to receive a balanced diet of God's Word.

### 26. What are some things we can do to make the public reading of Scripture more meaningful?

One of the exciting developments in worship in the Christian Reformed Church is an increased emphasis upon careful preparation for the public reading of Scripture. The Reformed tradition has a high view of Scripture as the inspired Word of God. How fitting that we carefully prepare for the public reading of Scripture! This applies not only to the reading of Scripture before the sermon but also to all reading of Scripture. Here are some suggestions:

- Encourage your pastor or others who read the Scripture to read the passage aloud several times. Oral reading shows the reader where decisions have to be made about what a verse actually means, who is saying what, which words to emphasize, where to pause, and so forth.

- Identify one person in your congregation who has the gift of reading Scripture effectively and who can identify and cultivate that same gift in others. Through this person, develop a list of five to twenty readers. Use people who do a good job of reading. Seek to use people in this way who not only have the potential but also are not involved in worship leadership in any other ways. (If Marilyn already sings solos, don't ask her to read.) Scripture reading is one way young people can be meaningfully used in worship on a regular basis instead of just in an annual youth service.

- Use different people to represent different characters in the passage being read. Consider John 21:15-25, where Jesus reinstates Peter after Peter's denial of Jesus, asking Peter three times, "Do you love me?" Having three people read this Scripture (narrator, Jesus, Peter) can make this Scripture reading a powerful experience. (See *The Dramatized New Testament [NIV]* and *The Dramatized Old Testament [NIV]* edited by Michael Perry; published by Baker. These two volumes present most of Scripture in parts for such readings.)

- Memorize Scripture. All by itself, reciting Scripture from memory does not guarantee effective communication of Scripture. But when committing Scripture to memory is combined with these other ways of preparing for the presentation of Scripture, we can expect the Holy Spirit to use such diligent work in mighty ways.

**27. Recently I worshiped in a church where baptism took place after the sermon. That was new to me. Should baptism be celebrated before or after the sermon? Does it make any difference?**

Liturgical arguments can be made for either placement. Like holy communion, baptism can be understood as a response to the proclaimed Word of God and placed after the sermon. It can also be argued that the dying and rising in Christ that are signified in baptism very naturally are linked to the service of confession of sin and assurance of pardon earlier in the service. The goal here should not be to declare one place in the liturgy to be the only appropriate place for baptism. The goal rather is to think through the placement. Different services may even call for different placements.

Very practical concerns also come into play in these kinds of decisions. For example, in the case of infant baptism, parents would probably prefer to have the baptism before the sermon so they don't have to worry about their baby squawking and squealing all the way through the sermon. But an adult baptism may fit very beautifully after the sermon. Another consideration is whether the church wants other children from the congregation to be present for baptism. Many congregations with children's worship programs prefer to do the baptism service before the younger children leave for children's worship so that the children can witness the baptism. These may seem like mundane considerations to one who is concerned only about liturgical arguments. But liturgy and worship involve real people, and it is fitting that all of these things be weighed when such liturgical decisions are made.

**28. We realize that the mood of holy communion should be one of celebration, not mourning. What suggestions do you have for helping us accomplish that?**

We offer three suggestions:

- First, worship leaders and the church as a whole must truly believe that God intends for communion to be a celebration. Beyond that, the leaders of the communion liturgy must lead with vitality and enthusiasm. Pastors must be reminded to lead the communion liturgy as though it were the first and last communion liturgy they will ever lead.

- Second, churches should strongly consider the revised liturgical forms for communion, which are less didactic and more celebrative and participatory than earlier forms (see *Agenda of Synod 1994*, pp. 166-191; forms are also available on computer disk from CRC Publications).

- Third, worship leaders should not necessarily aim for every communion service to have the same mood. Communion takes place in the larger context of worship. Communion on Easter Sunday should have a different mood than communion on New Year's Eve does. Especially as congregations celebrate communion more frequently, they must strive to make each celebration of communion fit in a particular service and season of worship. Music selection within the communion liturgy is probably the biggest variable in making a particular communion service fit into the broader worship service of which it is a part.

**29. As elders we have been discussing how often we should celebrate holy communion. Some say the Bible teaches that communion was celebrated weekly. Others say that's not so. How often should we celebrate communion?**

There is good biblical and historical support for communion being a more regular part of Christian worship than it has been in the Christian Reformed Church. Most CRC congregations celebrate communion between four and twelve times a year. It's probably safe to say that most churches that have changed the frequency of communion have increased its frequency. Certainly the argument that more frequent communion diminishes its impact is a weak argument. That seems to be an argument against weekly preaching and even against worship itself.

We advise you to talk with churches that have gone to more frequent communion. You will gain a lot of wisdom and insight from churches that already have struggled with these issues. It seems fair to generalize that churches that have moved toward more frequent communion have done so with great blessing and have seldom returned to a pattern of less frequency.

Sometimes worship leaders contend that there is a conflict between frequent celebration of holy communion and sensitivity to seekers at worship. There is certainly an inherent *otherness* to holy communion, if for no other reason than the fact that only those who are part of the body of Christ may participate in the celebration. Holy communion accentuates the wall between belief and unbelief, between being part and not being part of the body of Christ. Yet, for these very reasons, there is also something powerfully evangelistic about holy communion. In holy communion, the gospel message becomes visible in powerful ways. We would prefer to think of the relationship between frequent celebrations of holy communion and sensitivity to the seeker at worship not as one of conflict but of creative tension.

**30. Our pastor is really uptight about making too many announcements in church. What can we do to help him relax about this?**

Don't give him so many announcements. Announcements are not worship. People don't come to church to hear about the Building Committee meeting Monday night. They come to worship God. Your pastor dislikes announcements for good reasons.

It would be nice if announcements were not necessary, but they are. And sometimes they even communicate things about the broader ministry and community life of the church that indirectly give worship a fuller ministry context. Even so, the following rules should govern announcements:

- Don't repeat what's already in the bulletin.

- Make sure it's necessary to make an announcement. (In an age of telephones, the meeting of a committee that has only four members should not have to be announced.)

- Carefully think through when you want to make announcements. Some congregations prefer to do all the announcements at one time in the service, probably before the pastoral prayer, when some pastoral concerns may also be announced. Other congregations make congregational announcements toward the end of the service as part of the offertory—emphasizing the offering of one's life to God through the activities of the community.

- Be concise.

(For a more extensive discussion of announcements in worship, we refer you to *Lift Up Your Hearts,* CRC Publications, p. 7.2.)

# REFERENCES

Best, Harold. *Music Through the Eyes of Faith.* San Francisco: Harper, 1993.

Calvin, John. *Institutes of the Christian Religion,* ed., John T. McNeill. Philadelphia: Westminster, 1960.

Cornwall, Judson. *Meeting God.* Altomonte Springs: Creation House, 1986.

Dawn, Marva. *Reaching Out Without Dumbing Down: A Theology of Worship for the Turn-of-the-Century Church.* Grand Rapids: Eerdmans, 1995.

Flannery, Austin, ed. *Vatican Council II: The Conciliar and Post Conciliar Documents.* Collegeville: The Liturgical Press, 1978.

Gilquist, Peter. *Becoming Orthodox: A Journey to the Ancient Christian Faith.* Brentwood: Wolgemuth and Hyatt, 1989.

"Guidelines and Forms for the Sacraments," *Agenda for Synod 1994.* Grand Rapids: CRC Publications, 1994.

Hayford, Jack. *Worship His Majesty.* Waco: Word Books, 1987.

The Heidelberg Catechism. *Psalter Hymnal.* Grand Rapids: CRC Publications, 1987.

Johanssen, Calvin M. *Music and Ministry: A Biblical Counterpoint.* Peabody: Hendrickson Publishers, 1984.

Keiffert, Patrick R. *Welcoming the Stranger: A Public Theology of Worship and Evangelism.* Minneapolis: Fortress Press, 1992.

Lewis, C. S. *Letters to Malcolm: Chiefly on Prayer.* New York: Harcourt, Brace & World, 1964.

MacGregor, Geddes. *The Rhythm of God.* New York: Seabury Press, 1974.

Morgenthaler, Sally. *Worship Evangelism: Inviting Unbelievers into the Presence of God.* Grand Rapids: Zondervan, 1995.

Old, Hughes Oliphant. *Themes and Variations for a Christian Doxology: Some Thoughts on the Theology of Worship.* Grand Rapids: Eerdmans, 1992.

*Our World Belongs to God, A Contemporary Testimony.* Study Edition. Grand Rapids: CRC Publications, 1987. (Also in *Psalter Hymnal,* 1987.)

Perry, Michael. *The Dramatized New Testament.* Grand Rapids: Baker Books, 1993.

———. *The Dramatized Old Testament.* Grand Rapids: Baker Books, 1996.

Peterson, David. *Engaging with God: A Biblical Theology of Worship.* Grand Rapids: Eerdmans, 1992.

Peterson, Eugene. *Earth and Altar: The Community of Prayer in a Self-Based Society.* Downers Grove: InterVarsity Press, 1985.

Postman, Neil. *Amusing Ourselves to Death: Public Discourse in the Age of Show Business.* New York: Viking, 1985.

"Report of Liturgical Committee," *Acts of Synod 1968.* Grand Rapids: CRC Publications, 1968.

Schmemann, Alexander. *For the Life of the World: Sacraments and Orthodoxy.* Crestwood: St. Vladimir's Seminary Press, 1988.

Schuller, Robert. *Your Church Has a Fantastic Future! A Possibility Thinker's Guide to a Successful Church.* Ventura: Regal Books, 1986.

Senn, Frank. *The Witness of the Worshiping Community.* New York: Paulist Press, 1993.

Webber, Robert. *Signs of Wonder: The Phenomenon of Convergence in Modern Liturgical and Charismatic Churches.* Nashville: Abbott Martyn Press, 1992.

Westermeyer, Paul. "The Future of Congregational Song." *The Hymn* (Vol. 46, No. 1), January, 1995.

White, James F. *Sacraments as God's Self-Giving.* Nashville: Abingdon Press, 1983.

———. *Introduction to Christian Worship.* Nashville: Abingdon Press, 1980, revised edition 1990.

Wolterstorff, Nicholas. *Until Justice and Peace Embrace.* Grand Rapids: Eerdmans, 1983.

# ADDITIONAL RESOURCES FOR STUDY AND PLANNING

---

## HISTORY, THEOLOGY, AND PRACTICE

Best, Harold. *Music Through the Eyes of Faith.* San Francisco: Harper San Francisco, 1993.

*Thought-provoking ideas about music, worship, and the Christian life.*

Dawn, Marva. *Reaching Out Without Dumbing Down: A Theology of Worship for the Turn-of-the-Century Church.* Grand Rapids: Eerdmans, 1995.

*A provocative call to keep worship free from cultural captivity.*

Hustad, Donald. *Jubilate II: Church Music in Worship and Renewal.* Carol Stream: Hope Publishing, 1993.

*The most complete volume available on music in evangelical worship.*

McKim, Donald K., ed. *Major Themes in the Reformed Tradition.* Grand Rapids: Eerdmans, 1992.

*Stimulating reflections on what it means to be Reformed from leading thinkers in the tradition. See especially Nicholas Wolterstorff's substantial article "The Reformed Liturgy."*

Morgenthaler, Sally. *Worship Evangelism: Inviting Unbelievers into the Presence of God.* Grand Rapids: Zondervan, 1995.

*An argument for participatory and theologically coherent worship in the church-growth tradition.*

Ortiz, Manuel. *One New People: Models for Developing a Multiethnic Church.* Downers Grove, IL: InterVarsity Press, 1996.

*An excellent book dealing with different models in the development of churches with a multicultural focus; provides helpful distinctions between a multicultural and a multiethnic church.*

Peterson, David. *Engaging with God: A Biblical Theology of Worship.* Grand Rapids: Eerdmans, 1992.

*Probably the best recent study of what the Bible tells us about worship.*

Senn, Frank. *The Witness of the Worshiping Community: Liturgy and the Practice of Evangelism.* New York: Paulist Press, 1993.

*A critique of contemporary developments that calls the church to fulfill its mission through worship that is faithful to Scripture and the church's traditions.*

von Allmen, Jean-Jacques. *Worship: Its Theology and Practice.* New York: Oxford University Press, 1965.

*A classic study by an influential Swiss Reformed theologian [out of print].*

Webber, Robert, ed. *The Complete Library of Christian Worship.* Hendrickson Publishing, 1993-1995.

*This seven-volume set provides informative articles and resources (many by CRC authors) dealing with all aspects and traditions of worship. A good resource for well-endowed church libraries.*

White, James F. *Protestant Worship: Traditions in Transition.* Louisville: Westminster/John Knox Press, 1989.

*A good resource for locating Reformed worship within the larger Protestant tradition.*

Benedict, Daniel C. and Craig K. Miller. *Contemporary Worship for the 21st Century: Worship or Evangelism?* Nashville: Discipleship Resources, 1994.

*Includes model services and commentary illustrating various ways of integrating traditional and seeker emphases.*

———. *Book of Common Worship.* Louisville: Westminster/John Knox Press, 1993.

*This Presbyterian worship book provides a wealth of useful material adaptable to almost any worship occasion. Also includes the* Revised Common Lectionary.

Bower, Peter C. *Handbook for the Revised Common Lectionary.* Louisville: Westminster/John Knox Press, 1996.

*The three-year cycle of the* Revised Common Lectionary *includes synopsis of all Scripture passages with anthem suggestions, psalmody settings, organ music, and hymns.*

Old, Hughes Oliphant. *Leading in Prayer: A Workbook for Worship.* Grand Rapids: Eerdmans, 1995.

*Sound advice, biblical reflections, and practical examples of the various types of prayers offered in public worship.*

Pederson, Steve, ed. *Sunday Morning Live: A Collection of Drama Sketches from Willow Creek Community Church.* Grand Rapids: Zondervan, 1992-94.

*This six-volume series sets the standard for seeker-oriented drama.*

Perry, Michael, ed. *The Dramatized New Testament (NIV).* Grand Rapids: Baker Books, 1993. *The Dramatized Old Testament (NIV).* Grand Rapids: Baker Books, 1996.

*These two volumes present most of Scripture in parts for dramatized readings.*

*Psalter Hymnal Handbook.* Grand Rapids: CRC Publications, 1998.

*Backgrounds and liturgical suggestions for every song and brief biographies of every author and composer in the 1987* Psalter Hymnal; *also essays on the history of congregational song.*

*Reformed Worship.* Grand Rapids: CRC Publications (published quarterly).

*An indispensable journal for worship leaders and committees seeking practical assistance in planning, structuring, and conducting congregational worship.*

*Revised Common Lectionary.* The Consulation on Common Texts, 1992. Published by Wood Lakes Books (Canada) and Abingdon Press (United States).

*The Consulation on Common Texts (CCT) is an ecumenical group to which the CRC belongs. The lectionary is also included within the* Book of Common Worship *and* Handbook to the Revised Common Lectionary.

*Songs for LiFE.* Leader's Edition. Grand Rapids: CRC Publications, 1995.

*A children's hymnal that includes a complete worship education program and suggestions for planning children's worship times.*

*So You've Been Asked To . . . Be a Soloist, Develop a Worship Team, Lead in Prayer, Present a Children's Message, Prepare a Choral Reading, Read Scripture.* Grand Rapids: CRC Publications, 1996.

*This series of pamphlets helps members prepare and lead the congregation in worship and other areas.*

Stewart, Sonja M. and Jerome W. Berryman. *Young Children and Worship.* Louisville: Westminster/John Knox, 1989.

*Probably the most influential current model for designing children's worship.*

Vanderwell, Howard D. and Norma deWaal Malefyt. *Lift Up Your Hearts: Resources for Planning Worship.* Grand Rapids: CRC Publications, 1995.

*A practical resource (loose-leaf binder) loaded with information and tips for planners and worship leaders, much of it compiled from Reformed Worship and other CRC sources.*

## AUDIOVISUAL RESOURCES

*Blended Worship: A Guide to Blending the Old and the New.*

A six-part audiotape with worship samples by Robert Webber, one of the best-known proponents of *convergence* worship. Might be used in conjunction with one of Webber's many recent books including *Renew Your Worship: A Study in Blending of Traditional and Contemporary Worship* and *Blended Worship: Achieving Substance and Relevance in Worship* (both Peabody: Hendrickson Publishers, 1996). See also the interview with Robert Webber in *Reformed Worship,* 39, March 1996, pp. 3-5. This audiotape series and all of Webber's books are available from the Institute for Worship Studies, Box 894, Wheaton, IL 60189 (phone 630-510-8905).

*Developing Dynamic Worship.* Lynn Likkel and Alvin J. Vander Griend. Grand Rapids: CRC Publications, 1995.

*A three-hour video seminar with resources for worship leaders.*

*An Inside Look at the Willow Creek Seeker Service: Show Me the Way* and *An Inside Look at the Willow Creek Worship Service: Building a New Community.* Grand Rapids: Zondervan, 1992.

*Video presentations (each 116 minutes) of a Willow Creek seeker service and believer service featuring interviews with senior pastor Bill Hybels and staff members. Available from TRAVARCA at 1-800-968-7221.*

*The Lay Liturgist: The Oral Reading of Scripture in Worship.* West Ottawa, MI: BBC Communications, 1993.

*A 20-minute video on effective Scripture reading, with interactive leader's guide. Available from TRAVARCA at 1-800-968-7221.*

*Liturgy and Life: A Reformed Understanding of Worship.* Grand Rapids: Reformed Church in America, 1996.

*A 26-minute video that provides background information and theological reflections on the important elements of worship. Available for purchase from the RCA at 1-800-968-7221 or for rent from TRAVARCA at 1-800-968-7221.*

*The Meaning of Mystery: Baptism and Communion.* Louisville/Grand Rapids: Presbyterian and Reformed Educational Ministries, 1992.

*A 45-minute video on the theology and practice of the sacraments, with leader's guide. Available from TRAVARCA at 1-800-968-7221.*

---

## INTERNET RESOURCES

---

Those with access to the Internet can tap an enormous reservoir of material, from worship resources to discussion groups on virtually every aspect of liturgy, music, and evangelism. Some possible starting points for exploring this ever-changing field are listed below.

*Reformed Worship:* http:\\www.reformedworship.org

*Features excerpts from the current issue of this quarterly journal and subscription information. Watch for updates and links to other worship sites.*

*CRC Publications:* http:\\www.crcpublications.org

*Highlights selected curriculum resources, resources for congregational ministry (including those for music and worship), and training and consulting services (including children and worship training) currently listed in the agency's catalog.*